A TREATISE ON TREATIES

UNDERSTANDING CANADA

A TREATISE ON TREATIES

CROWN-INDIGENOUS TREATIES IN CANADIAN LAW

Bryan Birtles

UNIVERSITY OF TORONTO PRESS
Toronto Buffalo London

INSTITUTE OF PARLIAMENTARY AND POLITICAL LAW
INSTITUT DE DROIT PARLEMENTAIRE ET POLITIQUE

© University of Toronto Press 2024
Irwin Law
An imprint of University of Toronto Press
Toronto Buffalo London
utorontopress.com

ISBN 978-1-5522-1730-6 (paper)   ISBN 978-1-5522-1731-3 (PDF)

Cataloguing in Publication available from Library and Archives Canada

Cover image: Adobe Stock

We wish to acknowledge the land on which the University of Toronto Press operates. This land is the traditional territory of the Wendat, the Anishnaabeg, the Haudenosaunee, the Métis, and the Mississaugas of the Credit First Nation.

University of Toronto Press acknowledges the financial support of the Government of Canada and the Ontario Arts Council, an agency of the Government of Ontario, for its publishing activities.

**Canada Council
for the Arts**

**Conseil des Arts
du Canada**

ONTARIO ARTS COUNCIL
CONSEIL DES ARTS DE L'ONTARIO
an Ontario government agency
un organisme du gouvernement de l'Ontario

Funded by the
Government
of Canada

Financé par le
gouvernement
du Canada

Canadä

For J.H. and R.M.

Contents

Foreword

During his academic preparation for the practice of law, Bryan Birtles became interested in the complex legal aspects of the relationship between that part of the population of Canada comprised of those now called settlers and the Indigenous peoples, who inhabited this area earlier than the settlers' arrival. He pursued this interest during articling and is now in the same field of practice, seemingly his chosen career path. This constant attention has enabled him to claim the label of expert. With the present book, he is both enhancing his own expertise and fostering the knowledge of the Canadian population at large, in respect of his area of specialization.

Canada is today acknowledged to be a constitutional democracy. Indeed, that is the bedrock of the *Understanding Canada* collection. In that context, the first important revelation for readers of this volume in the collection is that several treaties between the colonizers and the Indigenous peoples predate more comprehensive and better-known constitutional documents. Whether or not these instruments that are the focus of this book are categorized as being "constitutional" in nature, they evidently constitute part of the legal foundation upon which Canada is built. In that sense alone, they are worthy of attention. There is far more.

Treaties are not only historical. The treaty-making process inside Canada continues and is likely to remain a feature of the political-legal scene. In a system of government comprising a federal authority, ten provinces and three territories, the need, the ability, and the desire to engage in treaties infuses a degree of flexibility and practicality into the country's structure of government and its processes of governance. Opinions may differ on the role of treaties in the modern legal fabric of Canadian society. Some may see treaties as fusing individual Indigenous communities into the overall governmental network of Canada. Others may perceive the practice of treaty-making as improving governance through flexibility, based on local status and conditions. Whatever perspective the reader chooses to adopt, the greatest certainty rising from this book is that expanding the bounds of knowledge and attention is both necessary and beneficial. Whether one reads this book in the home of an Indigenous community, a government office, or the office of a Bay Street law firm seeking to arrange further investment and development, information and interpretation are essential aspects of knowledge relevant to our own society.

A Treatise on Treaties: Crown-Indigenous Treaties in Canadian Law is, moreover, not entirely restricted to Canada. Comparisons are drawn from other jurisdictions that were settled from outside. That is an enormous benefit, as Canadian law and public policy operate not in a void but in a global framework. Familiarization with foreign models enables comment and comparison.

This book is written and published to assemble information and to enlighten the reader. It is a tool of knowledge and for increased knowledge. It will not right past wrongs. However, if it contributes to reconciliation, or at least to the development of a collaborative future, it will have amounted to a great success. Most importantly, we must note that there has been little, if any, specialized legal literature focused on Crown-Indigenous treaties in Canada. The addition of this book provides two services. First, it focuses attention on an underdeveloped domain of law. Most importantly, it focuses readers' attention on the reality that the legal system itself is an expanding universe.

Gregory Tardi
Editor, *Understanding Canada* collection
April 2024

Preface

My name is Bryan Birtles, and I am the son of Mark and Kathey Birtles. I was born in Calgary, raised in Edmonton, and now I live in Toronto. I am a settler, a Canadian of northern European ancestry.

The impetus for this book occurred while I was an articling student. I articled at the Ontario Superior Court of Justice in Toronto as a clerk, where I was privileged to be involved in a case that consisted of a novel claim for Aboriginal title to submerged land, as well as a claim for treaty breach. Unusually, and luckily, I worked on the case for my full term as a clerk; most articling students at the court are reassigned halfway through the term in order to maximize their experiences. I was also lucky to see the end of the case — which at least four other clerks had worked on over the preceding years — with the decision finally published on one of my last days at the court.

I did countless hours of research into treaties, especially into fulfillment and breach. The research covered much of Canada's jurisprudence on the subject and touched on the United States', Australia's, South Africa's, and New Zealand's approaches to treaties and Indigenous law as well. At one point, perhaps frustrated by the difficulty in finding an answer to what seemed to be a straightforward question, the judge I was working for lamented that there was no equivalent to *Chitty on Contracts* or *Wigmore on Evidence* for Crown-Indigenous treaties in Canada. She suggested that, with the amount of research I had already completed to that point, I was in as good a position as anyone to write such a book. So I did, and this is it.

As an analogue to *Chitty on Contracts* or *Wigmore on Evidence*, this book is designed to be what lawyers call a doctrinal or "black letter" law book. Although I have no doubt that some opinion or editorializing is present, the intention is simply to describe the law as it is, to help judges and lawyers in Canada efficiently solve legal questions having to do with the formation, implementation, and breach of Crown-Indigenous treaties in Canada. People who write books on Indigenous or Aboriginal law in Canada often have an activist's perspective, and their work has influenced me significantly. But I have made a conscious effort to keep this book wedded directly to the jurisprudence to make it as practical as possible for both activists and non-activists working in Aboriginal law in Canada.

Treaties are the foundation of our country, more so even than the Constitution. After all, without access to land and resources — which treaties provided — there would be nothing for me and my fellow settlers to constitute. On this basis, they are worthy of the detailed consideration by the legal profession that the Constitution has received since Confederation. But if you flip ahead and look at the length of this brief treatise, you would have to conclude that either I have left out a lot of law or there just isn't that much law to begin with. Rest assured that I have been as inclusive as possible; there just isn't that much law. Another intention of this book is that putting all of this law in one place will encourage more, and more thoughtful, consideration of the law of Crown-Indigenous treaties in Canada.

This book would be nothing without the people who taught me. First and foremost, Professor Karen Drake, a member of the Wabigoon Lake Ojibway Nation, had the most significant impact on me as a student at Osgoode Hall Law School. She infused Indigenous law into every aspect of her teaching, including in subjects as dry as civil procedure, and encouraged me to pursue knowledge and experience in both Indigenous and Aboriginal law. Second, I want to thank the Honourable Wendy Matheson of the Ontario Superior Court of Justice, who pushed me to delve as deeply as possible into the jurisprudence and encouraged me to write this book. I also want to thank the members of the Osgoode Indigenous Students Association — especially Isaac Twinn from Sawridge First Nation — from whom I learned so much in my time at law school. Finally, I would like to acknowledge the judges and my fellow lawyers on the legal counsel team at the Specific Claims Tribunal of Canada, as well as the citizens of every First Nation I have been privileged enough to visit in the course of my work, from whom I learn every day.[*]

I want to acknowledge as well the people who most encouraged me to go to law school and who encouraged and supported me while I was there and in my legal career: my wife Jenny Huntley, my aforementioned parents, all of my family, and my friends Ken Munro and Danielle Sandhu.

Bryan Birtles
Toronto, 2024

---

[*] This ought to go without saying, but this treatise is written in my personal capacity. It does not necessarily reflect the opinions of my employer.

"Hold the paper up to the light
(some rays pass right through)."

—TALKING HEADS

CHAPTER ONE

On the Nature of Treaties

A Working Definition of Treaties in Canada

Although it is something of a paradox, the sensible place to begin developing a definition of "treaty" in Canada is with what treaties are not: treaties are not contracts.[1] Despite being "analogous" to contracts,[2] and despite the Supreme Court of Canada (SCC) utilizing contractual principles to interpret treaty agreements,[3] if there is one thing we know about treaties between the Crown and Indigenous Nations in Canada, it is that they are not contracts.

So what are they? Treaties are agreements that "create enforceable obligations based on the mutual consent of the parties."[4] There is an element of a mutually beneficial exchange occurring, typically an exchange of land for guaranteed rights, as in *Mikisew Cree First Nation v Canada (Governor General in Council)*.[5] But many earlier treaties were exchanges of significantly less objective value: peace in exchange for trade, for example, as the treaty at issue in *R v Marshall* was determined to be,[6] or peace and alliance in exchange for safe passage, religious liberty, and trade, as the treaty in *R v Sioui* was determined to be.[7]

From the above, we may be tempted to conclude that a treaty is simply an enforceable, mutually beneficial exchange. This is not satisfactory, however, because this is, essentially, the definition of a contract.[8] And if we know nothing else about treaties in Canada, we at least know the one thing they are not: contracts. Something more is necessary before we arrive at an acceptable working definition.

The element of time, this treatise suggests, is the fundamental difference between a treaty and a contract: unlike contracts, treaties are intended to last forever. In some cases, the treaty itself is explicit on the point. In Treaty No. 45½, for example, the Saugeen Ojibway Nation exchanged 1.5 million acres of land in 1836 for a promise to protect "for ever" the Nation's remaining territory from the "encroachments of the whites," who were swiftly moving into the region.[9] Another good example is Treaty No. 4, where, in the midst of negotiations in 1874 at Fort Qu'Appelle, Saskatchewan, the Crown's chief negotiator Alexander Morris remarked:

> [T]he promises we have to make to you are not for to-day but for tomorrow, not only for you but for your children born and unborn, and the promises we make will be carried out as long as the sun shines above and the water flows in the ocean.[10]

Further evidence of the long-term nature of treaty agreements in Canada stems from *Sioui*. At issue in that case was a document that, at first glance, appears to be nothing more than a safe passage, provided by Brigadier General James Murray to a group of French-allied Huron near the end of the Seven Years' War. These warriors had switched allegiance to Britain, and General Murray's document guaranteed a safe passage from the site of their surrender to their home territory. However, the document also guaranteed "the free exercise of religion, customs and trade with the English," something the SCC remarked "cannot but raise serious doubts" that the document was *merely* a safe passage.[11] In *Sioui*, the Court concluded that the document — created in 1760 — could support a treaty right to practise ancestral customs on public property more than two centuries later.[12] The Court was adamant about the treaty's continuity: despite the Crown's argument that the treaty was extinguished due to disuse over the intervening years, the Court ruled that "a solemn agreement cannot lose its validity merely because it has not been invoked."[13]

One final point is important: treaties are international agreements because they were, and are, concluded between *nations*. They are not regarded as interstate treaties under Canadian law, however, and are therefore not interpreted via international legal principles.[14] At times in the jurisprudence, these agreements between nations within what is now Canada are referred to as "domestic" treaties, but this nomenclature is both inappropriate for being incorrect and disrespectful to Indigenous signatories, who never gave up their sovereignty.[15] The division between international treaty interpretation principles and Canadian jurisprudence's treaty interpretation principles is further explored in Chapter 2.

From all of the above, we arrive at the working definition that must be borne in mind throughout the remainder of this treatise. The definition contains three elements: treaties in Canada are *international agreements*, providing *mutual benefit* to each party, that last *forever*.

The Relationship Between Treaties and Canadian Law

Treaties have been referred to as the "legal basis to foster a positive long-term relationship between Aboriginal and non-Aboriginal communities"[16] and, at least outside a courtroom, have been called "the legal and constitutional foundation" of Canada.[17] Despite this level of importance, treaties intersect with Canadian law at only two points, although these intersections are significant. These points are section 88 of the *Indian Act*[18] and section 35 of the *Constitution Act, 1982*.[19]

The *Indian Act*

Section 88 of the *Indian Act* reads:

> Subject to the terms of any treaty and any other Act of Parliament, all laws of general application from time to time in force in any province are applicable to and in respect of Indians in the province, except to the extent that those laws are inconsistent with this Act or the *First Nations Fiscal Management Act*, or with any order, rule, regulation or law of a band made under those Acts, and except to the extent that those provincial laws make provision for any matter for which provision is made by or under those Acts.[20]

The practical effect of section 88 is twofold: first, despite section 91(24) of the *Constitution Act, 1867* making provinces incapable of legislating for Indigenous peoples,[21] section 88 extends the reach of provincial legislation of general application to Indians and First Nations; second, and more importantly for the purposes of this treatise, section 88 exempts from such laws of general application any conduct exercised as a treaty right. Again, as with many aspects of treaty interpretation, courts have taken a generous view of what a treaty "right" entails. This has meant that rights under treaty are not restricted "only to rights created by a Treaty" but include rights created, excepted, reserved, or confirmed by a treaty.[22]

As a practical and preliminary matter, to have any effect under section 88 of the *Indian Act*, the agreement at issue must be found to be a "treaty" under Canadian law. Where there is any doubt, this determination is accomplished via the *Sioui* test, discussed below in the section entitled "Treaty Formation and the Existence of a Treaty."

Another important preliminary matter is the definition of a provincial law of general application. In *Kruger et al v The Queen*, Dickson J (as he then was) offered the following definition:

> There are two *indicia* by which to discern whether or not a provincial enactment is a law of general application. It is necessary to look first to the territorial reach of the Act. If the Act does not extend uniformly throughout the territory, the inquiry is at an end and the question is answered in the negative. If the law does extend uniformly throughout the jurisdiction the intention and effects of the enactment need to be considered. The law must not be "in relation to" one class of citizens in object and purpose. But the fact that a law may have graver consequence to one person than to another does not, on that account alone, make the law other than one of general application. There are few laws which have a uniform impact. The line is crossed, however, when an enactment, though in relation to another matter, by its effect, impairs the status or capacity of a particular group.[23]

Most typically, section 88 of the *Indian Act* is used as a defence to regulatory prosecutions, especially when individuals fall afoul of fishing or hunting regulations. In *R v White*, one of the Douglas treaties — which promised the Saalequun Tribe the right to continue to "hunt for food over the land" it had sold to the Hudson's Bay Company — removed two accused from the ambit of British Columbia's *Game Act*.[24] Despite having been found with six deer carcasses out of season and without a permit, the accused were acquitted, the court determining that the *Indian Act*'s guarantee of treaty rights superseded provincial limitations to those rights.[25] A similar result occurred in *Sioui*, where members of the Huron Nation were accused of harvesting trees in contravention of provincial regulations applying to a national park.[26] In *R v Morris*, the SCC made a fine distinction when it came to hunting at night: a complete prohibition on hunting at night in British Columbia's *Wildlife Act* violated a treaty right promised to the Saanich Nation to be "at liberty to hunt over the unoccupied lands; and to carry on our fisheries as formerly" because the Saanich had hunted at night with illumination "from time immemorial."[27] However, an impugned prohibition on hunting dangerously did not violate the treaty; the Court rested its reasoning on the "common intention of the parties," concluding that "no treaty confers on its beneficiaries a right to put human lives in danger" and that such a limitation was in the interests of the personal safety of all residents of British Columbia, Indigenous and settler.[28]

The defence is not limitless. Courts have determined that treaty rights can be regulated and restricted under the *Badger* test, which this treatise discusses in Chapter 3.

It is not solely the rights contained within a treaty that are protected under section 88 of the *Indian Act*, however; a number of cases confirm that any conduct necessarily incidental to the exercise of a treaty right is similarly guaranteed. In *R v Sundown*, this included the right to build a log cabin as an incident of the right to hunt.[29] In *Simon v The Queen*, the Court determined that a right to possess a shotgun and ammunition was "reasonably incidental" to the right to hunt.[30] *Sundown* imports a reasonable person test to the question of an incidental right, stating, "A reasonable person apprised of the traditional expeditionary method of hunting would conclude that for this First Nation the treaty right to hunt encompasses the right to build shelters as a reasonable incident to that right."[31]

Furthermore, treaty rights are not static. In *Simon*, the SCC was called upon to interpret a 1752 treaty that guaranteed the right to hunt and fish "as usual" to Mi'kmaq signatories. Despite the fact that methods of hunting had advanced considerably by 1985, when the case was decided, Dickson CJ determined that "the inclusion of the phrase 'as usual' appears to reflect a concern that the right to hunt be interpreted in a flexible way that is sensitive to the evolution of changes in normal hunting practices."[32]

Although section 88 of the *Indian Act* restricts the application of provincial laws that violate treaty rights, prior to 1982, the federal government could write statutes that violated treaty rights with near impunity. In *Rex v Syliboy*, decided in 1929, the Nova Scotia County Court determined that a validly enacted statute of general application prevailed over treaty promises.[33] As late as the *Simon* case, determined in 1985, the SCC continued to hold that "when the terms of a treaty come into conflict with federal legislation, the latter prevails, subject to whatever may be the effect of s. 35 of the *Constitution Act, 1982*."[34] The effect of section 35 on treaty rights was determined in *R v Badger*, which imported the *Sparrow* justification test for Aboriginal rights infringement into the sphere of treaty rights.[35] The effect of this decision has been to remove Parliament's unilateral power to infringe or abrogate treaty rights.

The *Constitution Act, 1982*

Section 35(1) of the *Constitution Act, 1982* reads:

> The existing [A]boriginal and treaty rights of the [A]boriginal peoples of Canada are hereby recognized and affirmed.[36]

In addition, section 35(3) confirms that this recognition and affirmation are not restricted to historical treaties but apply to any rights arising from land claim settlements, both historical and future.[37] Per *Quebec (Attorney General) v Moses*, modern treaties such as the James Bay and Northern Quebec Agreement are similarly affirmed and recognized by section 35.[38]

Although the enactment of section 35 had a far-reaching effect on the doctrine of Aboriginal rights in Canada, its effect on treaty rights, although significant, was not as extensive. The primary effect of section 35 on treaty rights has already been discussed in the previous section: as determined by *Badger*, the recognition and affirmation of treaty rights in section 35 removed the federal government's power under section 91(24) of the *Constitution Act, 1867* to unilaterally infringe or abrogate treaty rights.[39]

An interesting decision made by the framers of the *Constitution Act, 1982* was to put section 35 in part II of the Act, which had the effect of placing the rights affirmed by this section *outside* the *Canadian Charter of Rights and Freedoms* and therefore outside the limitation clause in section 1 of the *Charter*, which subjects the rights guaranteed within to "reasonable limits prescribed by law as can be demonstrably justified in a free and democratic society."[40] This reality was commented on by McLachlin J (as she then was), writing in dissent in *R v Van der Peet*:

> [I]n the case of [A]boriginal rights guaranteed by s. 35(1) of the *Constitutional Act, 1982* [*sic*], the framers of s. 35(1) deliberately chose not to subordinate the exercise of [A]boriginal rights to the good of society as a whole. In the absence of an express limitation on the rights guaranteed by s. 35(1), limitations on them under the doctrine of justification must logically and as a matter of constitutional construction be confined, as *Sparrow* suggests, to truly compelling circumstances, like conservation, which is the *sine qua non* of the right, and restrictions like preventing the abuse of the right to the detriment of the [N]ative community or the harm of others — in short, to limitations which are essential to its continued use and exploitation. To follow the path suggested by the Chief Justice is, with respect, to read judicially the equivalent of s. 1 into s. 35(1), contrary to the intention of the framers of the Constitution.[41]

Despite the reasonableness of this position, Lamer CJ's viewpoint won out: the rights affirmed in section 35 can be limited, although not by section 1 directly. Rather, they are limited by section 1's "judicial equivalent," the justificatory test determined in *R v Sparrow*.[42] And although *Sparrow* dealt with Aboriginal rights, its justificatory framework was expanded to include infringements of treaty rights in *Badger*.[43] Although an obvious tension exists between what appears to be a clear choice made by the framers of the Constitution and the judicial interpretation of section 35 by the SCC in *Van der Peet*, this determination has never been revisited. In one of Canada's most recent treaty infringement cases, *Yahey v British Columbia*, the Supreme Court of British Columbia approved of the *Sparrow* test for justification of an infringement, commenting:

> Aboriginal and treaty rights protected by s. 35(1) are, however, not absolute. While the *Constitution Act, 1982* protects against the infringement of Aboriginal and treaty rights, such rights may be infringed in certain circumstances, when justified.[44]

Both the *Sparrow* and *Badger* tests for infringement are discussed in greater depth in Chapter 3 of this treatise.

Although this tension deserves reconsideration by the courts, it does not detract from the importance of section 35 to the exercise of treaty rights. The constitutionalization of treaty rights provides stronger *de jure* protection to such rights by elevating them above mere statutory law and doing away with the federal government's ability to unilaterally infringe or extinguish them while also providing stronger *de facto* protection by drawing attention to their elevated status.

Types of Treaties

Even a casual glimpse at the jurisprudence will make it glaringly apparent that there is more than one "type" of treaty in Canada. At the very least, treaties can be divided between historical treaties and modern ones, the James Bay and Northern Quebec Agreement being considered the "pioneer" in the latter field.[45] Other writers have suggested up to six different types of treaty within Canada, half of which do not involve the Crown at all.[46] This treatise is concerned solely with treaties between the Crown, in any of its guises, and Indigenous Nations in what is now known as Canada and therefore categorizes treaties into three types based on both their impetuses and their eras: (1) the peace and alliance era, from approximately 1700 to 1812; (2) the "Deal Terms" era of 1812 to 1921; and (3) the reconciliation era from 1975 to the present.

In the peace and alliance era, no territory was ceded; each party received benefits typically in the nature of peace, trade, and protection from enemies. Both parties benefitted from the exchange of goods, and European parties aided Indigenous allies against enemies both European and Indigenous, whereas Indigenous parties aided their European allies in the same manner. A good example of the peace and friendship treaties is the series of treaties entered into between the British Crown and a number of Mi'kmaq communities in Nova Scotia in 1760 to 1761. Under these treaties, the British were promised peace, which included promises not to disturb British settlements, not to entice soldiers to desert, to return prisoners, to refrain from taking "private revenge" in the event of any misunderstanding, and to cease trade with Britain's enemies; the Mi'kmaq, for their part, were promised truckhouses at which they could trade for goods and the implicit right to harvest materials for which the British would be willing to trade.[47] Another good example is the Covenant Chain, an alliance relationship established between the British and the Haudenosaunee Confederacy — also known as the Iroquois Confederacy or the Six Nations Confederacy — in the early seventeenth century and later extended to include the Anishinaabe and other nations as well. The Ontario Superior Court of Justice described the alliance created by the Covenant Chain as follows:

> The alliance was represented symbolically as a ship tied to a tree, first with a rope and then with an iron chain. The rope represented an alliance of equals; the iron represented strength. The iron chain became one of silver, a metal more durable and more beautiful than iron. The metaphor associated with the chain was that if one party was in need, they only had to "tug on the rope" to give the signal that something was amiss, and "all would be restored."[48]

The Covenant Chain also shows that the eras of treaty making are not discrete; there is inevitable overlap. The relationship created by the alliance continued to be important until well into the "Deal Terms" era, as defined here. Not only was the Covenant Chain alliance with Indigenous Nations instrumental in repelling the Americans in the War of 1812, the assistance of Indigenous warriors was also "repeatedly recalled" long after the war ended.[49] As late as 1849, Indian Superintendent

Thomas Anderson presented Anishinaabe Chief Shingwaukonse and Chief Tagawinini with medals for their services in the war.[50] This treatise uses the phrase "Deal Terms" era to emphasize that the benefits of these treaties have been interpreted by courts as being essentially restricted to the terms of the deal,[51] although courts have allowed for some evolution to protect the expectations of each party as the context has shifted.[52] Essentially, this era of treaty making concentrated on land cessions exchanged for the terms and rights offered within the treaty.[53] The best examples of this type of treaty are the numbered treaties of western Canada. Although this era of treaty making clearly benefitted the European and later the Canadian party more than their Indigenous counterparts — Canada is, after all, the second-largest land mass in the world — the treaties were entered into from the Indigenous perspective for an identifiable benefit: at the very least, there was an expectation that some land would be protected from incoming settlers in exchange for surrendering the rest of it and for the "guarantees" the Court speaks about in *Mikisew Cree*, guarantees that meant, at least to Indigenous beneficiaries, that they would be able to continue traditional activities over both reserved and ceded territory (where it had not been put to a "visible, incompatible" use)[54] and to live a traditional life.[55]

Finally, the reconciliation era or the era of modern treaties. These agreements are significantly different from those that came before in the sense that they are "meticulously negotiated by well-resourced parties"[56] and are significantly longer and more comprehensive than any other type of treaty.[57] For this reason, courts have identified a need to pay closer attention to the written terms of the agreements, in a departure from "traditional" treaty interpretation principles.[58] Nevertheless, these are agreements that provide benefits to each party: the Indigenous party may gain title to some areas of their traditional territories and enumerated rights over the rest of it, may gain procedural rights in terms of consultation and jurisdiction, and may even gain monetary settlements for past infringements, whereas the government gains certainty about title to the land and an enumerated process for decision making regarding the territory and may quiet title to any lands not reserved to the Indigenous party through the process.[59]

Capacity to Enter into Treaty

As noted in *Sioui*, the capacity of the parties to enter into a treaty is a preliminary matter.[60] As the Court commented, "If any one of these parties was without such capacity, the document at issue could not be a valid treaty and it would then be pointless to consider it further."[61] This reasoning is the flipside of that of the Court of Appeal in British Columbia in *Sga'nism Sim'augit (Chief Mountain) v Canada (Attorney General)*, which held that "[t]reaty rights owe their validity to agreement and it is unnecessary specifically to identify their source provided that the parties have the capacity to enter the agreement."[62]

It has been held in Canadian jurisprudence that the only parties capable of concluding a treaty of the type considered by this treatise are the Crown and Indigenous Nations.[63] Treaties between states that do not include an Indigenous party, even if they have an effect on Indigenous rights, are not treaties for the purposes of section 35 of the *Constitution Act, 1982*[64] or for the purposes of section 88 of the *Indian Act*.[65] That said, Canadian courts have long taken a generous approach to "agents" of the Crown, determining that such agents need not be connected directly to the Crown itself. In *White*, the court determined that the Hudson's Bay Company, having been made "lord of the lands in the Northwest Territories and Vancouver Island" under the company's charter, were capable of binding the Crown and concluding treaties, at least as late as 1854.[66]

To determine whether a party has capacity, a court must assume that the document in question "possesses the characteristics of a treaty and that the only issue that arises concerns the capacity of the parties to create obligations of the kind contained in a treaty."[67] In viewing the capacity of a European or Canadian party to a treaty with Indigenous peoples in North America, "the question of capacity must be seen from the point of view of the Indians at that time, and the Court must ask whether it was reasonable for them to have assumed that the other party they were dealing with had the authority to enter into a valid treaty with them."[68] *Sioui* sets a standard: representing "the British Crown in very important, authoritative functions" would make it reasonable on the part of Indigenous signatories to "assume [an individual] had the capacity to enter into a valid treaty with them."[69]

The capacity of the Indigenous party has not been a consistent doctrine within Canadian jurisprudence. One of the earliest cases to consider Indigenous capacity to enter treaty is *Syliboy*, determined by the Nova Scotia County Court in 1929.[70] The court concluded that the document in question was not a treaty because, as an "uncivilized people," the Indigenous party lacked the "rights of sovereignty" necessary to treat with another "civilized nation."[71] This reasoning was reversed by the SCC in *Simon*, where the Court determined, "Such language is no longer acceptable in Canadian law," and, furthermore, the judgment's "conclusions on capacity are not convincing."[72] In *Simon*, the capacity of the Indigenous party is founded on being representative of an identifiable group. Discussing a treaty between the Crown and the Mi'kmaq (spelled "Micmac" in the decision), the Court commented, "The Micmac Chief and the three other Micmac signatories, *as delegates of the Micmac people*, would have possessed full capacity to enter into a binding treaty on behalf of the Micmac."[73] This reasoning is echoed in *Sioui*, which determined that negotiation between Crown representatives and "Eight Sachems, of different nations, lately in alliance with the enemy, [who] have surrendered, *for themselves and their tribes*," was an integral aspect of determining that the document in question was indeed a treaty.[74]

As Canadian jurisprudence has continued to evolve, the capacity of Indigenous peoples to enter into treaty has come to be, essentially, presumed in the absence of evidence otherwise. The capacity of the Indigenous parties forms no part of the analysis in *Marshall No 1* or in *Badger, Mikisew Cree*, or *Moses*. This presumption may be linked to the evolution of the SCC's view of the purpose of treaties in the context of the reconciliation era, which encourages liberal and generous interpretation of treaties in an effort to encourage "a mutually respectful long-term relationship" between Indigenous peoples and the Canadian state.[75] On the same basis, it would be reasonable to presume Crown capacity in the absence of evidence to the contrary.

Land cession is not a requirement for finding a valid treaty, nor is it necessary for the Indigenous party to have Aboriginal rights arising from prior occupation of traditional territory in order to enter into a treaty. For example, in *Sioui*, the Huron signatories made treaty with the British outside traditional Huron territory in an effort to return to it safely, and the SCC found that entering into the agreement outside traditional Huron territory had no effect on the validity of the treaty.[76]

As a preliminary issue, capacity to enter into treaty is not a particularly difficult hurdle. For decades, Canadian courts have demanded very little evidence of capacity to clear this requirement. This is likely connected to the context in which these treaties were made and the way in which they are interpreted by Canadian courts. In *Simon*, Dickson CJ quoted with approval an article by N.A.M. MacKenzie that appeared in the *Canadian Bar Review* in 1929, criticizing the Nova Scotia County Court's decision in *Syliboy*, which stated:

> Ordinarily "full powers" specially conferred are essential to the proper negotiating of a treaty, but the Indians were not on a par with a sovereign state and fewer formalities were required in their case. Governor Hopson was the representative of His Majesty and as such had sufficient authority to make an agreement with the Indian tribes.[77]

From this we can be certain that the capacity to enter into a treaty between the Crown and Indigenous peoples in Canada is not the same as the capacity to enter into a treaty between two sovereign states. Like many aspects of Aboriginal law in Canada, treaties are *sui generis* agreements that fall "somewhere between the kind of relations conducted between sovereign states and the relations that such states had with their own citizens."[78]

Treaty Negotiation

Although this treatise will devote space at length to the doctrine of the honour of the Crown in relation to treaty interpretation and fulfillment, a brief word is necessary at this point regarding treaty negotiation and its relationship to the honour of the Crown. The honour of the Crown is a long-standing principle of Canadian jurisprudence, emerging at least as early as 1895, when Gwynne J of the SCC wrote:

> [T]he terms and conditions expressed in [treaties] as to be performed by or on behalf of the Crown, have always been regarded as involving

a trust graciously assumed by the Crown to the fulfilment of which with the Indians the faith and honour of the Crown is pledged, and which trust has always been most faithfully fulfilled as a treaty obligation of the Crown.[79]

Although Gwynne J wrote these words in dissent, they were subsequently adopted by the SCC in *Marshall No 1* in 1999. In that decision, the SCC held that the Crown's honour is "always at stake in its dealings with [A]boriginal people,"[80] which is, essentially, what gives rise to the application of the honour of the Crown during the negotiation process; despite the fact that an agreement has yet to be reached, negotiation is a "dealing" between the Crown and an Aboriginal people. Other decisions reinforce the idea that the honour of the Crown applies within the context of a negotiation. In *Haida Nation*, the SCC determined that the honour of the Crown "infuses the processes of treaty making and treaty interpretation. In making and applying treaties, the Crown must act with honour and integrity, avoiding even the appearance of 'sharp dealing.'"[81]

The honour of the Crown in the context of treaty negotiations does not belong solely to the federal Crown, despite section 91(24) of the *Constitution Act, 1867* giving sole legislative authority over "Indians, and Lands reserved for the Indians" to the federal government. Where treaty negotiation is conducted in a tripartite structure between the federal government, a provincial government, and an Indigenous Nation — as is often the case in modern treaty negotiations — the honour of the Crown applies to all aspects of Crown authority, both in right of Canada and in right of a province.[82]

It should be borne in mind that the honour of the Crown does not impose a duty to negotiate but that, having agreed to negotiate, the honour of the Crown dictates that the negotiation process be conducted in good faith.[83] The duty to negotiate in good faith, however, does not impose a duty to agree or even to conclude a treaty. Either party may terminate the process at will.[84]

The content of good faith within the context of a treaty negotiation is, at minimum, a lack of fraud or misrepresentation,[85] sufficient disclosure of relevant information,[86] honesty about potential outcomes of the negotiation,[87] and the absence of "sharp dealing" or oblique motive.[88]

Treaty Formation and the Existence of a Treaty

The test for the formation of a treaty between the Crown and an Indigenous people in Canada stems from *Sioui*. The flexible approach the SCC has dictated for treaty interpretation has similarly been dictated for the test to determine the existence of a treaty.[89] The test has three steps:

A treaty is characterized by:
1. The intention to create obligations
2. The presence of mutually binding obligations
3. A certain measure of solemnity[90]

As a preliminary matter to this test, however, the capacity of the parties to enter into treaty may need to be ascertained, the considerations for which are analyzed above.

Jurisprudence pre-dating *Sioui* continues to have an impact on the test, as this section will show. The analysis in *Sioui* applies to all three types of treaties identified in this treatise: the treaties of peace and friendship, the land-cession treaties, and modern treaties.[91]

The Intention to Create Obligations

In *Sioui* itself, the SCC held up the case *Regina v Taylor and Williams* as a source of factors to help a trier of fact determine whether or not a treaty exists.[92] Although *Taylor and Williams* was an interpretation case, the SCC commented that "the factors mentioned may be just as useful in determining the existence of a treaty as in interpreting it," and, in particular, "they assist in determining the intent of the parties to enter into a treaty."[93] There are five such factors identified in *Taylor and Williams* and restated in *Sioui*, although there is no reason to conclude that the list is exhaustive:

1. Continuous exercise of a right in the past and at present,
2. The reasons the Crown made a commitment,

3. The situation prevailing at the time the document was signed,
4. Evidence of relations of mutual respect and esteem between negotiators, and
5. The subsequent conduct of the parties.[94]

The facts of *Sioui* show how small a hurdle the first stage of the test is. It should be remembered that the document at issue in *Sioui* was incredibly short and resembled later treaties in almost no way. This is the entirety of the document:

> THESE are to certify that the CHIEF of the HURON tribe of Indians, having come to me in the name of His Nation, to submit to His BRITANNICK MAJESTY, and make Peace, has been received under my Protection, with his whole Tribe; and henceforth no English Officer or party is to molest, or interrupt them in returning to their Settlement at LORETTE; and they are received upon the same terms with the Canadians, being allowed the free Exercise of their Religion, their Customs, and Liberty of trading with the English: — recommending it to the Officers commanding the Posts, to treat them kindly.
>
> Given under my hand at Longueil, this 5th day of September, 1760.
>
> By the Genl's Command,
>
> JOHN COSNAN, JA. MURRAY.
> Adjut. Genl.[95]

The Crown in *Sioui* argued that this document was nothing more than a safe passage, given by General Murray in a personal capacity and therefore not binding on the Crown. This would certainly undercut the idea that the Crown had an intention to create obligations. However, extrinsic evidence showed not only the unique position of Indigenous Nations within the context of colonial North America in 1760 — unlike French settlers in North America, Indigenous Nations had the capacity to conclude treaties because their sovereignty was represented by leaders within the territory[96] — but also that this document, brief as it is, was the result of a day's negotiation between the parties and therefore was somewhat more than a unilateral safe passage: it was "the embodiment of an agreement reached between the representative of the British Crown and the representatives of the Indian [N]ations present."[97]

The first stage of the *Sioui* test may be a relatively easy one, but it should not be presumed. In *R v Vincent*, the Ontario Court of Appeal was called upon to determine whether the Jay Treaty — concluded between the newly formed United States and Great Britain in 1794, but without Indigenous signatories — conferred a right on Indigenous peoples to move large quantities of tobacco across the border without paying duties.[98] The right claimed by the accused stemmed from Article III of the treaty, which read:

> No Duty of Entry shall ever be levied by either Party on Peltries brought by Land or Inland Navigation into the said Territories respectively, nor shall the Indians passing or repassing with their own proper Goods and Effects of whatever nature, pay for the same any Impost or Duty whatever. But Goods in Bales, or other large Packages unusual among Indians shall not be considered as Goods belonging bona fide to Indians.[99]

The court drew a distinction between a treaty concluded by two states and one concluded by an Indigenous Nation and the Crown within British North America or, later, Canada. Only the latter are treaties under section 35 of the *Constitution Act, 1982*, the court concluded.[100]

Underlying this conclusion is, among other things, the *Sioui* test's first stage and the factors from *Taylor and Williams* as enumerated by the SCC. The court remarked that the first, second, and fifth factors are clearly not present in the Jay Treaty — that is, the right at issue was not continuously exercised before and after the treaty, the Crown made no commitment to an Indigenous Nation within the treaty, and the subsequent conduct of the parties did not belie a right conferred by the treaty.[101] With no intention to create obligations between the Crown and an Indigenous party, the court concluded that "the rights claimed by the appellant and the intervenors are not existing treaty rights recognized or confirmed by para. 35(1) of the *Constitution Act, 1982*."[102]

The Presence of Mutually Binding Obligations

Whereas the first stage of the *Sioui* test is a small but not presumable hurdle, once the first stage is passed — that is, a court finds an intention on both parties to create obligations — the second stage can very nearly be presumed. In *Sioui* itself, the Court concerned itself almost solely with the first and third parts of the test: finding an intention to create obligations, and with the obligations created having been set down in a document, the presumption of mutually binding obligations is made almost without comment, and the Court moved on to consider the solemnity of the agreement.[103]

A better place to look for the analysis of the second step of the *Sioui* test is *Moses*, which concerns a modern treaty, the James Bay and Northern Quebec Agreement. The question before the Court was whether this agreement — concluded more than half a century after the final numbered treaty — was a treaty for the purposes of section 35, although, atypically, this analysis occurs in the dissent and is simply adopted by the decision, which presumes the agreement to be a treaty.[104] The dissent, and therefore the Court, concluded that the agreement is indeed a treaty, relying heavily on the second stage of the *Sioui* test to conclude that it "establishes a comprehensive legal framework, setting out the parties' respective responsibilities where services and rights to land are concerned and organizing their relationships for the future."[105]

It should be borne in mind that it is not necessary for a treaty to resemble the "450-page legal document"[106] at issue in *Moses* for a court to be able to ascertain the presence of mutually binding obligations. In *Simon*, which heavily influenced the test established in *Sioui*, the SCC had to determine whether a 1752 agreement between the British and the Mi'kmaq was a treaty for the purposes of section 88 of the *Indian Act* and the purposes of section 35 of the *Constitution Act, 1982*. The agreement ended hostilities between the two groups, promised assistance from each party to the other in various ways, offered a mechanism for the resolution of future disputes, and promised the "free liberty of Hunting & Fishing as usual" to the Indigenous signatories.[107] Having reviewed these terms — all of which are contained in fewer than 900 words — the Court concluded:

The Treaty was entered into for the benefit of both the British Crown and the Micmac people, to maintain peace and order as well as to recognize and confirm the existing hunting and fishing rights of the Micmac. In my opinion, both the Governor and the Micmac entered into the Treaty *with the intention of creating mutually binding obligations* which would be solemnly respected.[108]

From these examples, it becomes clear that the second stage of the *Sioui* test is an extremely low hurdle: the presence of respective responsibilities that are the product of agreement between the parties — and not the product of unilateral imposition — will suffice to pass this stage of the test.

A Certain Measure of Solemnity

Solemnity is, like the presence of mutually binding obligations, not a large hurdle. In *Sioui*, determining that a measure of solemnity defines a treaty stems partly from an analysis of *White*, an appeal by the Crown to an acquittal for possessing game out of season.[109] This analysis continues to influence all aspects of the test for treaty formation, keeping low any claimant's burden of proving the existence of a treaty. In *White*, Lord JA wrote:

> "Treaty" is not a word of art and in my respectful opinion, it embraces all such engagements made by persons in authority as may be brought within the term "the word of the white man" the sanctity of which was, at the time of British exploration and settlement, the most important means of obtaining the goodwill and cooperation of the [N]ative tribes and ensuring that the colonists would be protected from death and destruction. On such assurance the Indians relied. In view of the argument before us, it is necessary to point out that on numerous occasions in modern days, rights under what were entered into with Indians as solemn engagements, although completed with what would now be considered informality, have been whittled away on the excuse that they do not comply with present day formal requirements and with rules of interpretation applicable

to transactions between people who must be taken in the light of advanced civilization to be of equal status.[110]

The "informality" of which Lord JA spoke no doubt contributed to the determination in *Sioui* that merely a "certain" measure of solemnity is required. As the Court commented in *Sioui*, the above passage "shows that formalities are of secondary importance in deciding on the nature of a document containing an agreement with the Indians."[111]

The concept of solemnity in treaty making also relates to the long-term practice of the Crown to engage with Indigenous Nations via the formalities of their own political cultures. As the court writes in *Chippewas of Sarnia Band v Canada (Attorney General)*:

> Formal meetings between Crown officials and First Nations were held at public Council meetings attended by the chiefs and other members of the First Nations. Certain formalities became an accepted part of these meetings and served to emphasize the nation-to-nation nature of the dealings. Many of those formalities reflected [A]boriginal customs and usages. The First Nations peoples attached considerable importance to compliance with these formalities and the Crown representatives were aware of the importance of these formalities to the First Nations.[112]

As this passage makes clear, the solemnity of a treaty-making occasion is connected, as well, to capacity: the capacity to bind a nation, European or Indigenous, is communicated to the other party through the solemnity of the occasion.

Although solemnity is a small hurdle, it should not be presumed: a party seeking to propound a treaty should come armed with evidence tending to show solemnity. The exchange of wampum is often relied upon to show solemnity,[113] as is negotiation preceding agreement,[114] especially accompanied by ceremony and formality and, in particular, the use of a pipe during discussions.[115]

Collective and Individual: The Nature of Treaty Rights

Primarily, treaty rights are collective rights: they inhere within the group as a whole, provided that ancestors of the group signed or adhered to the treaty at issue. However, typically, individuals within the group exercise these collective rights. The interplay between the group nature and the individual-within-a-group nature of treaty rights can be confusing, but *Sundown* provides a helpful framework.

Recall that in *Sundown*, the SCC needed to determine whether the building of a permanent log cabin in a provincial park was incidental to a right to hunt, as guaranteed by Treaty No. 6. Uncontroverted evidence had been presented at trial showing that the Cree Nation that pursued the case hunted in a style the Court called "expeditionary" and which it described this way:

> [A] hub-and-spoke style of hunting in which hunters set up a base camp for some extended period of time ranging from overnight to two weeks. Each day they move out from that spot to hunt. They then return to the base camp to smoke fish or game and to prepare hides.[116]

The Court determined that the *actual* historical practice of hunting was what was protected by the treaty; although the method could evolve — swapping out bows and arrows for shotguns and shells, for example, or evolving from moss-covered lean-tos to log cabins[117] — the methods themselves were the heart of what the treaty was intended to protect. The Court therefore defined an incidental right expansively, as "something which allows the claimant to exercise the right in the manner that his or her ancestors did, taking into account acceptable modern developments or unforeseen alterations in the right."[118]

Having determined that, in the context of Treaty No. 6, building a log cabin was reasonably incidental to the treaty-protected right to hunt, the Court then felt it necessary to define the contours of who held the right. Although the named defendant, John Sundown, certainly held the right, he did not hold it as an individual; rather, he had the right to build and utilize a log cabin as an incidental aspect of a right to hunt under Treaty No. 6, but only as a member of the Nation that was party to the treaty. The Court analogized the incidental right to property rights, saying:

> Any interest in the hunting cabin is a collective right that is derived from the treaty and the traditional expeditionary method of hunting.

It belongs to the Band as a whole and not to Mr. Sundown or any individual member of the Joseph Bighead First Nation. It would not be possible, for example, for Mr. Sundown to exclude other members of this First Nation who have the same treaty right to hunt in Meadow Lake Provincial Park.[119]

Therefore, Mr Sundown has a right to build and utilize such a cabin as an individual member of his Nation, but he holds this right collectively with all other members.

One consequence of the collective nature of treaty rights is the strict territoriality of most rights guaranteed by a treaty. Despite having the incidental right to build a log cabin in order to exercise the right to hunt in his Nation's traditional territory, Mr Sundown would not have the same treaty right to do so in territory covered by a different treaty or by no treaty. Unlike individual rights, collective rights are not portable.

The idea that treaty rights are collective rights over specific territory is supported by cases such as *R v Marshall* (*Marshall No 2*), where the SCC affirmed its decision in *Marshall No 1*, saying that in seeking to utilize a treaty right as a defence to a regulatory prosecution, a defendant must "demonstrate that he or she is a member of an [A]boriginal community in Canada with which one of the local treaties ... was made, and was engaged in the exercise of the community's collective right to hunt or fish in that community's traditional hunting and fishing grounds."[120]

The collective nature of treaty rights caused the Federal Court in *Gill v Canada* to rule that actions to enforce such rights cannot be undertaken as class proceedings because the *Class Action Rules* allow for an individual to opt out, writing:

[B]ecause a declaration as to [A]boriginal rights and treaty benefits is not a remedy of an individual nature, accruing to only those individuals who participate in the litigation, but a collective right, [they are] not amenable to opting out.[121]

In *Behn v Moulton Contracting Ltd*, the SCC was invited to determine directly the relationship between individual and collective aspects of

Aboriginal rights, a determination that would have been applicable to treaty rights as well. However, the Court found that it was not necessary to make such a determination, dismissing the case on the grounds of abuse of process instead.[122] The SCC did comment on a proposal made by the Grand Council of the Crees and Cree Regional Authority, which intervened in the case, calling it an "interesting suggestion":[123]

> [T]he interveners Grand Council of the Crees and Cree Regional Authority propose in their factum, at para. 14, that a distinction be made between three types of Aboriginal and treaty rights: (a) rights that are exclusively collective; (b) rights that are mixed; and (c) rights that are predominantly individual. These interveners also attempt to classify a variety of rights on the basis of these three categories.[124]

The SCC left for another day the balance between collective and individual rights in the context of Aboriginal and treaty rights, saying:

> It will suffice to acknowledge that, despite the critical importance of the collective aspect of Aboriginal and treaty rights, rights may sometimes be assigned to or exercised by individual members of Aboriginal communities, and entitlements may sometimes be created in their favour. In a broad sense, it could be said that these rights might belong to them or that they have an individual aspect regardless of their collective nature. Nothing more need be said at this time.[125]

It should be borne in mind, however, that some treaty rights have consistently been treated as individual rights. Although never made explicit in the jurisprudence, the dividing line appears to be the source of the right: where rights are *conferred* by treaty, courts show a willingness to treat them as individual rights; where rights are, instead, *confirmed* by treaty, courts are more likely to insist on their collective nature. This dividing line is also present in the court's treatment of the fiduciary duty in relation to treaty agreements, which this treatise addresses in Chapter 3.

For example, in *Papaschase Indian Band (Descendants of) v Canada (Attorney General)*, the trial judge remarked in *obiter* that the right to the payment of an annuity under a treaty is a right that accrues to an individual because, the court remarked, "If this sum was not paid, the individual band member could sue for it, and the right to collect it would pass to his or her heirs."[126] This view of treaty annuities as individual rights is treaty specific, however; in *Soldier v Canada (Attorney General)*, the Manitoba Court of Appeal held that, at least within the context of Treaty No. 1 and Treaty No. 2, which were at issue, annuity entitlements are individual rights. The court distinguished these rights from those confirmed in *Sundown*, saying:

> Unlike the right to hunt, which belongs to the band collectively, the right to this particular annuity belongs to each individual. The payments are not made to the band or to the chiefs. There is a specific benefit in a specific amount to be paid to members of the band as individuals. If a certain individual entitled to his or her annual treaty payment failed to retrieve that payment from the Crown, the First Nation was not provided with those funds. While Mr. Sundown could not exclude another member of the band from using the cabin, only Soldier or Bone could collect their particular annuity payment.[127]

The *Soldier* decision distinguishes between treaties such as the ones at issue and others that promise that "the annuities were to be paid 'to the said Chiefs and their tribes.'"[128] These, the court implied, can give rise to collective rights to annuity payments, based on the wording of the treaty. This conclusion was reinforced in *Restoule*, which considered both the Robinson-Huron and Robinson-Superior treaties' annuity provisions. It was determined that by the wording of the treaties — which promised an annual lump sum to be paid "to the Chiefs and their Tribes," as well as an augmentation clause that allows for increased payments to individuals[129] — these annuities were a collective, lump-sum entitlement with distribution conditions rather than separate collective and individual entitlements.[130]

Although it behooves the SCC to offer clarity on the issue of the nature of treaty rights, the binary between rights confirmed and rights conferred is a relatively safe assumption, barring any treaty language that insists on a collective conferred right.

Can Treaties End?

This treatise has only just defined treaties as "international agreements, providing mutual benefit to each party, that last forever," so it may seem strange to ask whether they can end. Nevertheless, the jurisprudence suggests that, under either historical or extraordinary circumstances, treaties can indeed end. The burden of proof that a treaty has been terminated lies with the party arguing for its termination.[131]

Historical Circumstances

In *Montana Band v Canada*, the Federal Court had to determine which of three First Nations — if any — held the beneficial interest in an Alberta-based reserve known as Indian Reserve No. 139.[132] The reserve was originally surveyed for the Bobtail Band in 1885,[133] led by Chief Bobtail, who adhered to Treaty No. 6 in 1877.[134] In 1885 and 1886, "members of the Bobtail Band including Chief Bobtail were granted discharges from treaty and took scrip," the court wrote.[135] Writing in the 1890s, the deputy superintendent general of Indian affairs, Hayter Reed, described the discharges as "exodus from Treaty" and said that, having done so, Chief Bobtail's Band had "forfeited title" to the reserve.[136]

It should be noted, of course, that this exodus did not end Treaty No. 6 itself. It persisted between Canada and the agreement's other Indigenous signatories, but Chief Bobtail's exodus would appear impossible under the law as it stands now. The Federal Court explained that, prior to the *Statute of Westminster*,[137] given royal assent in late 1931, the nature of treaties between the Crown and Indigenous peoples in Canada was different than it is today:

> Because Great Britain held sovereignty for Canada and the North-West Territories until 1931, Treaty 6 and the parties to it are subject to the rules of International Law respecting nation-to-nation agreements.[138]

The court determined that it was the international nature of the treaty that allowed for Chief Bobtail's discharge from the agreement and exodus from treaty. This suggests that, prior to 1931, treaties between the Crown and Indigenous peoples in Canada were the equivalent of interstate treaties, subject to international legal principles to which they are no longer considered to be.[139] The Federal Court of Appeal dismissed all appeals against the ruling in *Montana First Nation v Canada*.[140]

In the context of *Montana First Nation*, little turned on the idea that treaties in Canada were international in scope prior to the *Statute of Westminster*, and the court's comments should be considered *obiter dicta*. Nevertheless, they may prove consequential in the future.

Extraordinary Circumstances

At least two SCC decisions suggest that a treaty could end by hostilities: *Simon* and *Marshall No 1*.

In *Simon*, the Court had to consider whether a peace and friendship treaty signed between the Crown and the Mi'kmaq in 1752 was terminated by renewed hostilities that erupted in 1753, as the Crown argued.[141] The plaintiffs argued that, because the English "initiated the hostilities . . . therefore, the Crown should not be permitted to rely on them to support the termination of the Treaty."[142] The Court wrote that although both the First Nation and the Crown "looked to international law on treaty termination" in order to make their cases, in the context of *sui generis* Crown-Indigenous treaties in Canada, "these principles are not determinative."[143] The Court continued: "It may be that under certain circumstances a treaty could be terminated by the breach of one of its fundamental provisions" but that in the context of *Simon*, "inconclusive and conflicting evidence . . . makes it impossible for this Court to say with any certainty what happened on the eastern coast of Nova Scotia 233 years ago."[144] As the Crown had not met its evidentiary burden, the Court determined that "the Treaty of 1752 was not terminated by subsequent hostilities in 1753. The Treaty is of as much force and effect today as it was at the time it was concluded."[145]

In *Marshall No 1*, decided almost fifteen years following *Simon*, the Crown again tried to show that the same 1752 treaty had been terminated by hostilities, such that the plaintiff could not rely on it to ground a right to harvest and trade in eels without a licence.[146] The

Court commented that, at trial in *Marshall No 1*, "[t]he Crown led more detailed evidence of hostilities," and a reasonable inference is that the Crown may have been successful had the Court had to decide.[147] This did not come to pass, however, as the "evidence apparently persuaded the appellant at trial to abandon his reliance on the 1752 Peace and Friendship Treaty" in favour of later treaties, signed between 1760 and 1761, which managed to achieve the "elusive peace" the Treaty of 1752 could not.[148]

The jurisprudence shows that hostilities are capable of terminating treaties but that the standard of proof is relatively high, and courts are eager to avoid the issue if at all possible. The *Statute of Westminster*, referenced in *Simon*, may even have a role to play in this question as it would appear that the SCC was prepared to apply international legal doctrines to some extent to treaties formed and potentially terminated in the eighteenth century. But there has never been any suggestion that more recent hostilities, such as the Ipperwash Crisis, 1492 Land Back Lane, and others, have affected treaty agreements.

CHAPTER TWO

On the Interpretation of Treaties

Interpretive Principles

Because Crown-Indigenous treaties in Canada are *sui generis* legal instruments, they require *sui generis* principles of interpretation.[1] These principles were laid out at their most succinct in *R v Marshall* by McLachlin J (as she then was). Although she was writing in dissent in *Marshall No 1*, the nine principles she cited have since been fully adopted by the Supreme Court of Canada (SCC), which referred to them as "the most frequently cited summary of the relevant interpretive principles" developed by the Court.[2] These nine principles are as follows:

1. Aboriginal treaties constitute a unique type of agreement and attract special principles of interpretation.

2. Treaties should be liberally construed and ambiguities or doubtful expressions should be resolved in favour of the [A]boriginal signatories.

3. The goal of treaty interpretation is to choose from among the various possible interpretations of common intention the one which best reconciles the interests of both parties at the time the treaty was signed.

4. In searching for the common intention of the parties, the integrity and honour of the Crown is presumed.

5. In determining the signatories' respective understanding and intentions, the court must be sensitive to the unique cultural and linguistic differences between the parties.

6. The words of the treaty must be given the sense which they would naturally have held for the parties at the time.

7. A technical or contractual interpretation of treaty wording should be avoided.

8. While construing the language generously, courts cannot alter the terms of the treaty by exceeding what "is possible on the language" or realistic.

9. Treaty rights of [A]boriginal peoples must not be interpreted in a static or rigid way. They are not frozen at the date of signature. The interpreting court must update treaty rights to provide for their modern exercise. This involves determining what modern practices are reasonably incidental to the core treaty right in its modern context.[3]

This treatise will discuss each of these nine principles in turn.

Treaties as Unique Agreements

This treatise has discussed at some length the idea that treaties are not contracts — see Chapter 1 — but it is a point worth repeating. Although somewhat analogous to contracts, Crown-Indigenous treaties in Canada are unique or *sui generis* legal instruments. As the SCC wrote in *R v Sundown*:

> Treaties may appear to be no more than contracts. Yet they are far more. They are a solemn exchange of promises made by the Crown and various First Nations. They often formed the basis for peace and the expansion of European settlement. In many if not most treaty negotiations, members of the First Nations could not read or write English and relied completely on the oral promises made by the Canadian negotiators.[4]

One might even conclude that these three sentences underpin most, if not all, of the subsequent principles explicated by McLachlin J.

However, in addition to being unique in regard to contracts, Crown-Indigenous treaties in Canada are also unique in regard to other legal instruments known as "treaties" — those interstate treaties that often precipitate trade, establish international institutions, or end hostilities. In *Simon v The Queen*, the Crown argued that the 1752 treaty relied upon by the defendant to answer a regulatory prosecution for hunting out of season had been terminated by subsequent hostilities, a concept borrowed from international law. The SCC determined that reliance on international law concepts in the context of a Crown-Indigenous treaty in Canada was inappropriate:

> In considering the impact of subsequent hostilities on the peace Treaty of 1752, the parties looked to international law on treaty termination. While it may be helpful in some instances to analogize the principles of international treaty law to Indian treaties, these principles are not determinative. An Indian treaty is unique; it is an agreement *sui generis* which is neither created nor terminated according to the rules of international law.[5]

To understand why international treaty principles are considered inappropriate, we must consider the difference between a "nation" and a "state." Although described here and elsewhere as "international treaties," such instruments might be more correctly considered to be "interstate treaties" as they are typically concluded between or among states. With the assertion of sovereignty by the British over what is now Canada, British and Canadian law considered such sovereignty achieved: as the Privy Council held in *St. Catherine's Milling and Lumber Co v The Queen*, the assertion of sovereignty "vested in the Crown a substantial and paramount estate, underlying the Indian title, which became a *plenum dominium* whenever that title was surrendered or otherwise extinguished."[6] Despite retaining a national character, Indigenous Nations in Canada cannot conclude interstate treaties because they lack the requisite sovereignty, according to the Crown. There is considerable tension between the idea that an assertion of sovereignty gains complete sovereignty and the SCC's determination in *Calder et al v Attorney-General of British Columbia* that "when the settlers came, the Indians were there, organized in societies and occupying the land as their forefathers had done for centuries"[7] — a state of affairs that bears considerable similarities to sovereign possession. It behooves Canada's highest court to resolve this tension if "one of the fundamental purposes of s. 35(1)"[8] — the reconciliation of pre-existing Indigenous societies and the assertion of Crown sovereignty — is to be attained.

Liberal Construction and Ambiguity

The liberal construction of treaty terms and the resolution of any ambiguities in favour of the Indigenous parties is a long-standing interpretive principle. It appears to be based on the fact that the treaty parties did not share a common language or common understanding of the meaning of law. As the SCC writes in *R v Badger*:

> The treaties, as written documents, recorded an agreement that had already been reached orally and they did not always record the full extent of the oral agreement.... [T]he treaties were not translated in written form into the languages (here Cree and Dene) of the various Indian nations who were signatories. Even if they had been, it is unlikely that the Indians, who had a history of communicating only orally, would have understood them any differently. As a result, it is well settled that the words in the treaty must not be interpreted in their strict technical sense nor subjected to rigid modern rules of construction.[9]

We can see an example of the effect of the resolution of ambiguity in favour of Indigenous claimants in *R v Sioui*. As explained in Chapter 1, *Sioui* concerned a group of Huron accused of cutting down trees in a national park who relied on a document from 1760 — which the Crown disputed was a treaty — as a defence. The document resembled a safe passage more than it did a treaty, but an ambiguity was created by the inclusion of the sentence "they are received upon the same terms with the Canadians, *being allowed the free Exercise of their Religion, their Customs, and Liberty of trading with the English.*"[10] The presence of what is, arguably, a minor ambiguity caused the SCC to determine, "In our quest for the legal nature of the document of September 5, 1760, therefore, we should adopt a broad and generous interpretation of what constitutes a treaty."[11] Ultimately, the SCC concluded that the document was a treaty and that its terms had subsisted until the present day.[12]

The root of this principle is the lack of shared language and the unequal bargaining power of the parties to the agreement. For that reason, when it comes to modern treaties, this principle is significantly less important — and may even be inappropriate. Instead, the SCC has suggested the application of the third of McLachlin J's interpretive principles, common intentions, to resolve ambiguities rather than automatically resolving ambiguities in favour of the Indigenous party:

> When interpreting a modern treaty, a court should strive for an interpretation that is reasonable, yet consistent with the parties' intentions and the overall context, including the legal context, of the negotiations. Any interpretation should presume good faith on the part of all parties and be consistent with the honour of the Crown. *Any ambiguity that arises should be resolved with these factors in mind.*[13]

Although this passage makes clear that, in the case of modern treaties, ambiguities are not to be automatically resolved in favour of the Indigenous party, this does not affect the principle that the terms of the treaty are to be interpreted generously. The impetus for generous interpretation of modern treaties does not stem from the lack of shared language or literacy but, instead, from the "grand purpose" of section 35, which is the "reconciliation of Aboriginal and non-Aboriginal Canadians in a mutually respectful long-term relationship."[14] Despite the significant differences in context between historical and modern treaties, to effect this grand purpose requires a generous interpretation. The SCC stated it in this way:

> The modern treaties, including those at issue here, attempt to further the objective of reconciliation not only by addressing grievances over the land claims but by creating the legal basis to foster a positive long-term relationship between Aboriginal and non-Aboriginal communities. Thoughtful administration of the treaty will help manage, even if it fails to eliminate, some of the misunderstandings and grievances that have characterized the past. Still, as the facts of this case show, the treaty will not accomplish its purpose if it is interpreted

by territorial officials in an ungenerous manner or as if it were an everyday commercial contract. The treaty is as much about building relationships as it is about the settlement of ancient grievances. The future is more important than the past.[15]

Common Intentions and Reconciliation of Interests

This rule of interpretation appears to stem from the fact that treaties are negotiated agreements that confer mutual benefits; therefore, each party to the agreement must have had specific benefits in mind when they entered into negotiations and then the subsequent agreement. As the SCC writes in *Sioui*, "Even a generous interpretation of the document ... must be realistic and reflect the intention of both parties."[16] Where common intentions can be discerned from the historical record or via context, these identifiable intentions should be relied upon rather than entering into any discretion-laden analysis of what might be "realistic." In *Badger*, for example, the SCC wrote that the "report of the Commissioners who negotiated Treaty No. 8 on behalf of the government underscored the importance to the Indians of the right to hunt, fish and trap" over the surrendered territory, with the commissioners setting down the following in the report:

> Our chief difficulty was the apprehension that the hunting and fishing privileges were to be curtailed. The provision in the treaty under which ammunition and twine is to be furnished went far in the direction of quieting the fears of the Indians, for they admitted that it would be unreasonable to furnish the means of hunting and fishing if laws were to be enacted which would make hunting and fishing so restricted as to render it impossible to make a livelihood by such pursuits. But over and above the provision, *we had to solemnly assure them that only such laws as to hunting and fishing as were in the interest of the Indians and were found necessary in order to protect the fish and fur-bearing animals would be made, and that they would be as free to hunt and fish after the treaty as they would be if they never entered into it.*[17]

The SCC concluded, based on the clear importance of the right to harvest to the Indigenous signatories at the time the treaty was agreed to, that an appropriate interpretation — taking into account the need to resolve uncertainties in favour of the Indigenous party — would be the one that altered or modified the treaty right "as little as possible."[18]

Common Intentions and the Honour of the Crown

The honour of the Crown is an extremely important doctrine applicable to all aspects of Crown-Indigenous relations, including treaties. As the SCC wrote in *Badger*, "the honour of the Crown is always at stake in its dealing with Indian people. Interpretations of treaties and statutory provisions which have an impact upon treaty or [A]boriginal rights must be approached in a manner which maintains the integrity of the Crown."[19] This treatise will discuss, at length, the honour of the Crown in relation to treaty fulfillment and breach. But in terms of interpretation, one presumption appears to be of unique, perhaps sole, importance: the Crown, Canadian law will presume, intends to fulfill its promises.[20]

This presumption manifests itself by holding the Crown accountable for its obligations arising from treaty. Connected to the previous interpretive principle regarding common intentions, this presumption operates to ensure that Crown promises cannot be later minimized; there is no room for "sharp dealing" on the part of the Crown.[21] The Crown cannot say one thing and later claim to have meant something different. It cannot bait and switch.

The concept of an *intention* to fulfill Crown promises provides an important limitation to the effect of this interpretive principle. There may be times where a Crown promise cannot be fulfilled but where such failure does not amount to a breach of the honour of the Crown. This will occur where the Crown undertook diligent efforts to implement its promise but where circumstances made fulfillment unforeseeably difficult or impossible. As the SCC wrote in *Manitoba Metis Federation Inc v Canada (Attorney General)* regarding a constitutional obligation but equally applicable to treaty obligations:

> Not every mistake or negligent act in implementing a constitutional obligation to an Aboriginal people brings dishonour to the Crown.

Implementation, in the way of human affairs, may be imperfect. . . . Nor does the honour of the Crown constitute a guarantee that the purposes of the promise will be achieved, as circumstances and events may prevent fulfillment, despite the Crown's diligent efforts.[22]

Therefore, the presumption is merely that the Crown *intends* to fulfill its promises, which allows a court to take such promises at face value when determining the common intentions of the parties.

Sensitivity to Cultural and Linguistic Differences

This treatise has already touched upon the reasoning behind and potential effect of this interpretive principle. In *Badger*, the SCC acknowledged that the written versions of treaties were not only not the entirety of the agreement but were often not translated into an Indigenous language.[23] This practice has consistently left Indigenous signatories at a distinct disadvantage when it comes to enforcing the rights and promises contained in the treaties: not only does the common law appear to favour the idea of an "entire agreement" clause within the law of contract, extrinsic evidence of oral terms can also be difficult to come by or may be in a form — oral history — that the common law finds difficult to accept as it violates the rule against hearsay.

A variety of strategies and presumptions have arisen to help give effect to this principle of interpretation, including the relaxation of the rules of evidence in Aboriginal cases, where justified. These presumptions are discussed in the next section.

As an interpretive principle, however, this ought to be read in association with the others and serves most often as a reminder to apply flexibility at each stage of a court's reasoning, sensitive to the need for justice and reconciliation between Indigenous and settler societies. There is a limit to such flexibility, however. As the SCC put it in *R v Van der Peet*, although it is important to consider the Indigenous perspective when it comes to a rights claim, "that perspective must be framed in terms cognizable to the Canadian legal and constitutional structure."[24] This demand for a cognizable framing is a significant limit on the sensitivity to cultural difference that is available to the judiciary and a threat to reconciliation because it privileges the Crown perspective. It is also at odds with a later instruction in *Van der Peet* that "[t]rue reconciliation" places equal weight on the Aboriginal and common law perspectives.[25] It is not equal weight if one perspective must be subservient to the other.

A Natural Interpretation of the Treaty's Words

Obviously connected to the linguistic and cultural differences between the parties to a Crown-Indigenous treaty, this interpretive principle should also be read in tandem with the one that follows, which instructs courts to avoid technical or contractual interpretations of these agreements.

One important aspect of this principle is the inclusion of the words "at the time." This brings an element of historical context into the interpretive exercise. For example, in *Saugeen First Nation v The Attorney General of Canada* — which considered, among other things, the correct interpretation of promises made in Treaty No. 45½ — the fact that the earlier Treaty No. 45 had been made on the same day, in the same place, and with a separate but interconnected group of Anishinaabe caused the presiding judge to conclude that the earlier treaty was "particularly important context" for the interpretation of Treaty No. 45½.[26]

Avoid Technical or Contractual Interpretations

A further reminder that treaties are *sui generis* and not interpretable as contracts or interstate treaties, this interpretive principle is a call for flexibility and should be read in conjunction with the other principles, especially the preceding instruction to interpret the words of the treaty in the sense that they would naturally have held for the parties at the time.

It should be borne in mind that this principle is, in itself, flexible and reactive to context. In *Quebec (Attorney General) v Moses*, the SCC stated that technical or contractual interpretations may be appropriate when a court interprets modern treaty agreements:

> The text of modern comprehensive treaties is meticulously negotiated by well-resourced parties. As my colleagues note, "all parties to the

Agreement were represented by counsel, and the result of the negotiations was set out in detail in a 450-page legal document" (para.
118). The importance and complexity of the actual text is one of the
features that distinguishes the historic treaties made with Aboriginal
people from the modern comprehensive agreement or treaty, of which
the James Bay Treaty was the pioneer. We should therefore pay close
attention to its terms.[27]

This determination ought to serve as a reminder that all nine of
McLachlin J's interpretive principles are flexible and are to be applied
in the pursuit of justice and reconciliation to whatever degree best
promotes these dual principles.

Courts Cannot Exceed What Is Possible "On the Language"

Although courts go to great lengths to interpret treaties in a flexible
manner, there are limits. This limit relates to the aforementioned determination in *Sioui* that "[e]ven a generous interpretation of the document ... must be realistic and reflect the intention of both parties."[28]

The inclusion of the phrase "on the language" in this principle
could raise an objection that the SCC is privileging the written text
of the document over its oral terms, which, elsewhere, the SCC has
implied should be thought of as the agreement itself, with the written
text a mere record of the treaty that "did not always record the full
extent of the oral agreement."[29] A court should not privilege the written
text of the treaty but rather interpret the use of the word "language" in
this principle to encompass the oral terms as well as any extrinsic evidence about common intentions; a realistic interpretation using all the
available evidence of the agreement's terms ought to be the goal. This
is consistent with Binnie J's decision in *Marshall No 1*, where he wrote:

> "Generous" rules of interpretation should not be confused with a
> vague sense of after-the-fact largesse. The special rules are dictated by
> the special difficulties of ascertaining what in fact was agreed to. The
> Indian parties did not, for all practical purposes, have the opportunity
> to create their own written record of the negotiations. Certain assump-
> tions are therefore made about the Crown's approach to treaty making

(honourable) which the Court acts upon in its approach to treaty interpretation (flexible) as to the existence of a treaty ..., the completeness of any written record (the use, e.g., of context and implied terms to make honourable sense of the treaty arrangement) ..., and the interpretation of treaty terms once found to exist.[30]

Therefore, judges are not necessarily restricted to what is possible within the language of the treaty document but certainly are restricted to what is a reasonable interpretation of the language encompassing the document, the oral terms, the surrounding context, the discernable intentions of the parties, and the meaning of the words as understood by the parties at the time the agreement was made.

Treaty Rights Are Not Frozen

The interpretive principle that warns against "freezing" treaty rights in the form they took when the treaty was entered into is based primarily on two facts: first, that treaties are not contracts, and second, that Indigenous peoples were organized into societies with thousands of years of historical evolution prior to the assertion of European sovereignty.

This treatise has argued that the primary difference between treaties and contracts is that treaties between the Crown and Indigenous Nations in Canada cannot end. Therefore, unlike in contract law, it is imperative that evolution of treaty terms be "baked in" to the agreement to react to changing context and circumstances or risk creating absurd results.

Similarly, the prior evolution of Indigenous societies in what is now Canada militates in favour of treaty evolution. Although the jurisprudence sometimes refers to rights "arising"[31] from a treaty, a more accurate description, in many cases, comes from *Van der Peet*: treaties represent the crystallization of and confirmation by the Crown of pre-existing Aboriginal rights, whether to land or activities.[32] As these rights pre-existed and evolved prior to the making of the agreements that confirmed them, it would be unjust not to permit them to continue to do so.

Two examples may help illustrate the lengths to which treaty rights can evolve. In *Duke v Puts* — a defamation case without, it should be noted, any Indigenous parties but that concerned a pharmacist in rural Saskatchewan with a large Indigenous clientele — the Court of Queen's Bench had cause to describe the evolution of the "medicine chest clause" in Treaty No. 6. The original clause is almost startlingly perfunctory and reads:

> That a medicine chest shall be kept at the house of each Indian Agent for the use and benefit of the Indians at the direction of such agent.[33]

The court described the evolution of the medicine chest clause in Treaty No. 6 territory in this way, which was later adopted by the Saskatchewan Court of Appeal:[34]

> Under the laws of Canada, derived from a number of treaties with the First Nations, provision has been made for a "medicine chest." In Treaty No. 6 the wording was "A medicine chest shall be kept in the house of each Indian agent for the use and benefit of the Indians at the direction of such agent." In *Drever v. the King* (1935), Ex. Ct. (unreported) Mr. Justice Angers opined that "The Indians were to be provided with all the medicines, drugs or medical supplies which they might need, entirely free of charge." This broad interpretation of the medicine chest clause has drawn adverse comment ... but with the broad interpretation applied by the courts since the 1982 *Charter of Rights and Freedoms*, generous provision of the medicines, drugs and medical supplies free of charge has been the policy of the governments involved.
>
> In Broadview this has meant that the local doctors and druggists have taken the place historically occupied by the Indian agent. Both the case load of the doctors and the prescription business of the druggist are, to a large degree, derived from the requirements of the nearby reserves and payment is from the public purse.
>
> While the non-[N]ative population receives prescriptions from a formulary which is restricted, the formulary for the First Nations is much broader to the point where even bandages and many over-the-counter drugs are the subject of a prescription by a doctor, who charges for his attendance, and there is a dispensing fee for the druggist.[35]

There is a clear evolution here based on changing context: as the concept of "medicine" itself evolved beyond what it was in the nineteenth century when Treaty No. 6 was agreed to, the standard for fulfilling the treaty promise had to evolve as well. The promise did not change, but what was necessary to fulfill it certainly did.

In *Sundown*, the same treaty was at issue but concerned a different promise. Facing a regulatory prosecution for building a cabin in a provincial park, John Sundown relied on the hunting and fishing clause in Treaty No. 6 in an effort to remove himself from the ambit of provincial regulations, based on section 88 of the *Indian Act*.[36] He showed at trial that his ancestors had long hunted in what the Court called an "expeditionary" style and described this way:

> [A] hub-and-spoke style of hunting in which hunters set up a base camp for some extended period of time ranging from overnight to two weeks. Each day they move out from that spot to hunt. They then return to the base camp to smoke fish or game and to prepare hides.[37]

Despite the fact that the evidence showed that Mr Sundown's ancestors constructed or used dwellings significantly less permanent than the log cabin he had utilized, the SCC determined that the right to hunt contained within Treaty No. 6 protected the right to hunt in the method that the Indigenous signatories preferred, which meant that the construction of a log cabin was a permissible evolution of the method and, similar to the court in *Duke v Puts*, tied this evolution to changing context:

> A hunting cabin is, in these circumstances, reasonably incidental to this First Nation's right to hunt in their traditional expeditionary style. This method of hunting is not only traditional but appropriate and shelter is an important component of it. Without a shelter, it would be impossible for this First Nation to exercise its traditional method of hunting and their members would be denied their treaty rights to hunt. A reasonable person apprised of the traditional expeditionary method of hunting would conclude that for this First Nation the treaty right to hunt encompasses the right to build shelters as a reasonable incident to that right. The shelter was originally

a moss-covered lean-to and then a tent. It has evolved to the small log cabin, which is an appropriate shelter for expeditionary hunting in today's society.[38]

The generous evolution of treaty terms also applies to modern treaties, despite the acknowledgement by the SCC that "because the circumstances that support a generous interpretation of historical treaties do not always exist in the context of modern agreements, courts should not automatically take such an approach without first considering whether it is necessary."[39] The reason a generous evolution continues to be applicable to modern treaties is because the context always supports such an interpretation: as historical treaties evolve because they cannot end, modern treaties — often known as final agreements, which offers a hint as to their intended longevity — similarly do not end, so evolution is necessary to avoid absurdity. At the same time, context informs the scope and scale of evolution. As with the examples from *Sundown* and *Duke* above, it stands to reason that modern treaty terms are unlikely to evolve absent noticeable changes to the surrounding societal context. In such cases, courts are more likely to enforce the agreement as it was made, based on the principle that modern treaties were made in the absence of language barriers or unequal bargaining power.

Evidentiary Presumptions

Evidentiary presumptions are applied to treaties in order to facilitate interpretation. This subsection discusses four specific evidentiary presumptions:

- Extrinsic evidence
- Oral history
- Generous interpretation of evidence
- Implied terms

Extrinsic Evidence

Unlike in contract law, where extrinsic evidence is only permissible to settle a dispute where the contract contains ambiguity, when it comes to Crown-Indigenous treaties, "extrinsic evidence of the historical and cultural context of a treaty may be received even *absent* any ambiguity."[40] This is typically based on the reality that because the parties did not share a common language in concluding historical treaties, and Indigenous signatories did not have written language, oral terms form the heart of the treaty, and the written version, created by the Crown and requiring translation for Indigenous treaty partners, does not contain the whole of the agreement. As the SCC wrote in *Badger*:

> [W]hen considering a treaty, a court must take into account the context in which the treaties were negotiated, concluded and committed to writing. The treaties, as written documents, recorded an agreement that had already been reached orally and they did not always record the full extent of the oral agreement.... The treaties were drafted in English by representatives of the Canadian government who, it should be assumed, were familiar with common law doctrines. Yet, the treaties were not translated in written form into the languages ... of the various Indian nations who were signatories. Even if they had been, it is unlikely that the Indians, who had a history of communicating only orally, would have understood them any differently.[41]

There may be a limit to the presumptive use of extrinsic evidence when it comes to modern treaties, however. As the SCC wrote in *Marshall No 1*:

> "Generous" rules of interpretation should not be confused with a vague sense of after-the-fact largesse. *The special rules are dictated by the special difficulties of ascertaining what in fact was agreed to.* The Indian parties did not, for all practical purposes, have the opportunity to create their own written record of the negotiations.[42]

In *Moses*, one of the few SCC interpretations of a modern treaty, the Court emphasized the equality between the parties in terms of legal representation and the level of detail in the ensuing agreement.[43] Where the "special difficulties" present in *Marshall No 1* are absent, and where the Indigenous party to the agreement does have the opportunity to participate in the creation of the written record, there may be significantly less impetus to allow extrinsic evidence absent ambiguity.

Oral History

The rule against hearsay has been relaxed to some degree in litigation regarding Aboriginal or treaty rights, allowing for the reception of oral history, even when it is clear that such histories are interwoven with legend or political expression.[44] As the SCC determined in *Delgamuukw v British Columbia*, an Aboriginal title claim but equally applicable to treaty claims:

> Notwithstanding the challenges created by the use of oral histories as proof of historical facts, the laws of evidence must be adapted in order that this type of evidence can be accommodated and placed on an equal footing with the types of historical evidence that courts are familiar with, which largely consists of historical documents. This is a long-standing practice in the interpretation of treaties between the Crown and [A]boriginal peoples .... To quote Dickson C.J., given that most [A]boriginal societies "did not keep written records," the failure to do so would "impose an impossible burden of proof" on [A]boriginal peoples, and "render nugatory" any rights that they have .... This process must be undertaken on a case-by-case basis.[45]

Via this altered evidentiary rule, oral history — despite its hearsay nature — can be admitted for the truth of its contents and given independent weight even without corroboration in the written historical record. In fact, courts are expected to put "oral histories on an equal footing with historical documentary evidence" while ensuring that "equal footing does not mean preferential treatment."[46]

Like hearsay evidence, however, oral history evidence cannot be admitted where all markers of reliability are absent. Whereas the principled approach to hearsay demands "necessity and reliability"[47] for admittance, oral history is deemed to require only "usefulness and reasonable reliability."[48] As explained by McLachlin CJ in *R v Marshall; R v Bernard*, whereas "usefulness" is measured on the same standard as "necessity," "reasonable reliability" is a significantly more flexible standard:

> Usefulness asks whether the oral history provides evidence that would not otherwise be available or evidence of the [A]boriginal perspective

on the right claimed. Reasonable reliability ensures that the witness represents a credible source of the particular people's history. In determining the usefulness and reliability of oral histories, judges must resist facile assumptions based on Eurocentric traditions of gathering and passing on historical facts.[49]

To test reliability, courts often turn to the method of transmission of oral histories, placing these methods on something of a scale, with formalized processes engaged in by the community as a whole or by designated individuals being the most reliable. In *Delgamuukw*, for example, the evidence showed that the oral histories relied upon by the Gitksan and Wet'suwet'en Nations — known as *adaawk* and *kungax*, respectively — were repeated at important feasts throughout the year as part of a formalized ritual where "dissenters have the opportunity to object if they question any detail and, in this way, ... ensure the authenticity of the adaawk and kungax."[50] Where oral histories are transmitted with less formality, courts remain willing to admit such evidence, but less weight is likely to be given to it due to its decreased reliability.[51]

Generous Approach to Evidence

In addition to taking a generous approach to the rule against hearsay, courts have repeatedly taken a generous approach to all evidence presented by Indigenous claimants. Although she was speaking specifically about oral history, McLachlin CJ expressed this broad approach to all evidence in *Marshall and Bernard*, writing, "Underlying all these issues is the need for a sensitive and generous approach to the evidence tendered to establish [A]boriginal rights, be they the right to title or lesser rights to fish, hunt or gather."[52]

This approach follows from the SCC's earlier decision in *Van der Peet*. In that case, the Court offered an extremely broad accommodation to the evidence of Indigenous claimants, allowing a relaxation of any rule of evidence where evidentiary difficulties exist that stem from the clash between oral and written legal cultures:

> In determining whether an [A]boriginal claimant has produced evidence sufficient to demonstrate that her activity is an aspect of a practice,

custom or tradition integral to a distinctive [A]boriginal culture, a court should approach the rules of evidence, and interpret the evidence that exists, with a consciousness of the special nature of [A]boriginal claims, and of the evidentiary difficulties in proving a right which originates in times where there were no written records of the practices, customs and traditions engaged in. The courts must not undervalue the evidence presented by [A]boriginal claimants simply because that evidence does not conform precisely with the evidentiary standards that would be applied in, for example, a private law torts case.[53]

Like the presumptions regarding extrinsic evidence and the rule against hearsay, however, there are limits to this generous approach to evidence, based on its necessity to the pursuit of justice. Where a modern treaty is at issue, this generous approach may not be appropriate because the evidentiary difficulties described in *Van der Peet* are absent. Similarly, historical treaties could be thought of on a scale in terms of the available evidentiary record; a peace and friendship treaty from the mid-1700s may have less available historical context than Treaty No. 11, the final numbered treaty signed in 1921. Trial judges will need to balance their approach to the evidence of Indigenous parties based on the availability of such evidence: where it is absent or lacking, what evidence is ultimately presented must be interpreted generously, but where the historical record is robust and capable of expressing the Indigenous perspective of the treaty at the time of its agreement, the generous reception of evidence becomes less necessary.

Implied Terms

In *Marshall No 1*, the SCC made clear that the officious bystander test, a doctrine borrowed from contract law, applies to Crown-Indigenous treaties. In that case, Donald Marshall relied on a 1760 peace and friendship treaty between the British Crown and the Mi'kmaq as a defence against a regulatory prosecution for selling eels without a licence, fishing without a licence, and fishing during the closed season with illegal nets. He claimed that a term in the treaty allowed him to fish in the way that he had, but there was significant ambiguity about the meaning of the term. The term in question read:

And I do further engage that we will not traffick, barter or Exchange any Commodities in any manner but with such persons or the managers of such Truck houses as shall be appointed or Established by His Majesty's Governor at Lunenbourg or Elsewhere in Nova Scotia or Accadia.[54]

At the trial and subsequent appeal, each level of court read the right contained in the treaty narrowly, seeing it as merely a right to bring goods to trade at the truckhouses set up for the purpose, a right that ceased with the end of the truckhouse regime and a shift to different avenues of trade by the next decade.[55] The SCC interpreted the clause differently, however, relying on the officious bystander test to determine that the right to trade implied a right to harvest goods for trade:

> The law has long recognized that parties make assumptions when they enter into agreements about certain things that give their arrangements efficacy. Courts will imply a contractual term on the basis of presumed intentions of the parties where it is necessary to assure the efficacy of the contract, e.g., where it meets the "officious bystander test" …. Here, if the ubiquitous officious bystander had said, "This talk about truckhouses is all very well, but if the Mi'kmaq are to make these promises, will they have the right to hunt and fish to catch something to trade at the truckhouses?," the answer would have to be, having regard to the honour of the Crown, "of course." If the law is prepared to supply the deficiencies of written contracts prepared by sophisticated parties and their legal advisors in order to produce a sensible result that accords with the intent of both parties, though unexpressed, the law cannot ask less of the honour and dignity of the Crown in its dealings with First Nations.[56]

It is important to note, in the context of a Crown-Indigenous treaty, that the honour of the Crown applies to the officious bystander test. This implies a more generous interpretation of the test itself, leading to a broader officious bystander test than might be allowable in a civil contract dispute. As with all evidentiary presumptions discussed in this section, the limit to this generous interpretation remains the requirements of justice: courts are to use the officious bystander test to deliver justice rather than "after-the-fact largesse."[57]

Application to Territory

For the vast majority of treaties, the question of what territory the agreement applies to simply fails to arise; the treaty itself lays out the territorial parameters. Early treaties often laid out simple boundaries, whereas later treaties utilized metes and bounds. For example, in Treaty No. 45½, signed in 1836, the territorial application is written as so:

> I now propose to you that you should surrender to your Great Father the Sauking Territory you at present occupy, and that you should repair ... to that part of your territory which lies on the north of Owen Sound, upon which proper houses shall be built for you, and proper assistance given to enable you to become civilized and to cultivate land, which your Great Father engages for ever to protect for you from the encroachments of the whites.[58]

Slightly later, but in the same vicinity, the Robinson treaties utilized something more akin to metes and bounds, although not to the same precision as might be demanded in a contemporary real estate contract. For example, the Robinson-Huron Treaty, signed in 1850, surrenders

> the eastern and northern shores of Lake Huron, from Penetanguishine to Sault Ste. Marie, and thence to Batchewanaung Bay, on the northern shore of Lake Superior; together with the islands in the said lakes, opposite to the shores thereof, and inland to the height of land which separates the territory covered by the charter of the Honorable Hudson Bay Company from Canada; as well as all unconceded lands within the limits of Canada West to which they have any just claim.[59]

Similar metes and bounds are also present in the Douglas Treaties concluded on Vancouver Island. By the time Treaty No. 6 was signed in 1876, however, metes and bounds recognizable to contemporary lawyers were being utilized:

> Commencing at the mouth of the river emptying into the north-west angle of Cumberland Lake; thence westerly up the said river to its source; thence on a straight line in a westerly direction to the head of Green Lake; thence northerly to the elbow in the Beaver River; thence down the said river northerly to a point twenty miles from the said

elbow; thence in a westerly direction, keeping on a line generally parallel with the said Beaver River (above the elbow), and about twenty miles distant therefrom, to the source of the said river; thence northerly to the north-easterly point of the south shore of Red Deer Lake, continuing westerly along the said shore to the western limit thereof; and thence due west to the Athabasca River; thence up the said river, against the stream, to the Jaspar House, in the Rocky Mountains; thence on a course south-easterly, following the easterly range of the mountains, to the source of the main branch of the Red Deer River; thence down the said river, with the stream, to the junction therewith of the outlet of the river, being the outlet of the Buffalo Lake; thence due east twenty miles; thence on a straight line south-eastwardly to the mouth of the said Red Deer River on the south branch of the Saskatchewan River; thence eastwardly and northwardly, following on the boundaries of the tracts conceded by the several treaties numbered four and five to the place of beginning.[60]

Modern treaties contain descriptions of territory utilizing metes and bounds as well as longitude and latitude and are too detailed to be reproduced here. For example, the James Bay and Northern Quebec Agreement — the modern treaty at issue in *Moses* — has a description of the territory it applies to that is dozens of pages long.[61]

Where a treaty is silent about its territorial application, determining which territory it applies to is an interpretive exercise guided by the principles explicated in *Marshall No 1* by McLachlin J (as she then was), with special emphasis on the common intentions of the parties.[62] The onus is on the party propounding the treaty, typically a defendant to a regulatory prosecution, as was the case in *Sioui*.[63] The question must be approached "with the same generous approach" to evidence as other interpretive exercises, including the evidentiary presumptions enumerated in this chapter.[64] Historical context, the SCC has suggested, is likely to elicit the answer.[65] Having analyzed the intentions of each party in negotiating and agreeing to a treaty in the *Sioui* case, the SCC concluded:

> [I]n view of the absence of any express mention of the territorial scope of the treaty, it has to be assumed that the parties to the treaty of September 5 intended to reconcile the Hurons' need to protect the

exercise of their customs and the desire of the British conquerors to expand. Protecting the exercise of the customs in all parts of the territory frequented when it is not incompatible with its occupancy is in my opinion the most reasonable way of reconciling the competing interests. This, in my view, is the definition of the common intent of the parties which best reflects the actual intent of the Hurons and of Murray on September 5, 1760.[66]

Therefore, the territorial scope of the treaty was the entirety of the Huron territory as of 1760, but with the limitation that an inconsistent use by the Crown would negate the practice of the protected rights in a particular area.

Historical context can become especially important in determining a breach of treaty, a topic covered in detail in Chapter 4. In *Mikisew Cree First Nation v Canada (Minister of Canadian Heritage)*, the plaintiff argued that the proposed creation of a winter road through its reserve would injuriously affect its treaty rights to hunt and trap in the area, whereas the Crown argued that because only twenty-three square kilometres out of the 840,000 kilometres encompassed by Treaty No. 8 were being taken up, "this is not a case where a meaningful right to hunt no longer remains."[67] The SCC determined that "[t]his cannot be correct" and commented on the absurdity of such an argument:

> It suggests that a prohibition on hunting at Peace Point would be acceptable so long as decent hunting was still available in the Treaty 8 area north of Jasper, about 800 kilometres distant across the province, equivalent to a commute between Toronto and Quebec City (809 kilometres) or Edmonton and Regina (785 kilometres). One might as plausibly invite the truffle diggers of southern France to try their luck in the Austrian Alps, about the same distance as the journey across Alberta deemed by the Minister to be an acceptable fulfilment of the promises of Treaty 8.[68]

The SCC recognized that "location is important" when it comes to treaty rights, ruling that an Indigenous Nation should be able to meaningfully exercise its treaty rights within the ambit of its traditional territory and not be forced to travel long distances within the bounds of the treaty to do so.[69]

CHAPTER THREE

On the Fulfillment of Treaties

The fulfillment of treaties between the Crown and Indigenous Nations in Canada involves the invocation of a variety of related doctrines to test whether what was agreed upon has been delivered by each side. In general — and especially in regard to the numbered treaties of the Canadian West — the fulfillment of the Indigenous side of the bargain can be presumed. In *Mikisew Cree First Nation v Canada (Minister of Heritage)*, the Supreme Court of Canada (SCC) gave an indication of why Indigenous adherence to Treaty No. 8 can be presumed: the territory controlled by Indigenous Nations in 1899 when the treaty was signed was given up and has never been returned. The SCC wrote:

> Made in 1899, the First Nations who lived in the area surrendered to the Crown 840,000 square kilometres of what is now northern Alberta, northeastern British Columbia, northwestern Saskatchewan and the southern portion of the Northwest Territories. Some idea of the size of this surrender is given by the fact that it dwarfs France (543,998 square kilometres), exceeds the size of Manitoba (650,087 square kilometres), Saskatchewan (651,900 square kilometres) and Alberta (661,185 square kilometres) and approaches the size of British Columbia (948,596 square kilometres). In exchange for this surrender, the First Nations were promised reserves and some other benefits including, most importantly to them, the following rights of hunting, trapping, and fishing.[1]

Fulfillment by Indigenous Nations in other types of treaties is similarly presumed, on the basis of the power imbalance that existed and continues to exist between the treaty partners. The Indigenous signatories, the SCC appears to believe, have had no choice but to fulfill their side of the bargain, whereas it has long been within the power of the Crown to renege. This appears to be true even where the power balance between the treaty parties has shifted or wholly reversed. For example, in *R v Marshall*, the fact that the Mi'kmaq were "a considerable fighting force"[2] in 1760 when the treaty at issue was signed and "not people to be trifled with"[3] meant that the main benefit the British gained via the treaty was peace with the Mi'kmaq, who had previously been allied with the French.[4] The Court left open the idea that the treaty could have been terminated by hostilities subsequent to a peace treaty, but it appears simply to presume that the peace arrived at via the 1760 treaty subsisted.[5] This may simply be so in the absence of evidence to the contrary, or it may stem from the SCC's general presumption that Crown-Indigenous treaties persist forever, coupled with the contemporary power imbalance between the Crown and the Mi'kmaq, which has meant for more than a century that the Mi'kmaq have had little choice but to uphold their commitment to peace. Whatever the source of the presumption, there is an extremely high bar — perhaps an impossible one — for the Crown to argue that their Indigenous treaty partners have failed to fulfill the terms of the treaty, especially in relation to any land cession.

For that reason, the questions of fulfillment explored in this chapter focus almost entirely on Crown conduct.

The Honour of the Crown

The honour of the Crown is the most important doctrine within the realm of treaty fulfillment. It is a broad doctrine that inheres to all aspects of the Crown-Indigenous relationship and, unlike related doctrines such as the fiduciary duty, has almost no limit to its application. However, the practical effect of this broad application is minimal: breaches of the honour of the Crown — absent breaches of related doctrines — have yet to give rise to relief beyond declaratory relief and have never given rise to damages in Canadian jurisprudence. Although the jurisprudence hints that, in the right case, damages may be available, it offers little guidance as to what factors make a case the "right" one. Ultimately, the doctrine is not well defined beyond the need for representatives of the sovereign to behave honourably at all times so as to maintain the "integrity" of the Crown.[6] In *R v Badger*, the SCC provided clues to behavioural standards, insisting that "sharp dealing" by the Crown can never be sanctioned, and said, "It is always assumed that the Crown intends to fulfil its promises."[7] It does not go any further. In the more recent decision in *Manitoba Metis Federation Inc v Canada (Attorney General)*, the Court offered a broad but simplistic definition:

> The phrase "honour of the Crown" refers to the principle that servants of the Crown must conduct themselves with honour when acting on behalf of the sovereign.[8]

Although the doctrine takes its contemporary shape from a series of cases beginning with *Guerin v The Queen*,[9] its roots are much older. Legal scholars have identified a variety of potential sources of the doctrine, including the 1664 Treaty of Albany,[10] the assertion of sovereignty by the British Crown,[11] or even in pre-Norman England.[12] In Canadian jurisprudence, the concept makes its first appearance at the SCC in 1895 in the dissenting reasons of Gwynne J, who wrote that treaties between the Crown and Indigenous Nations "have always been regarded as involving a trust graciously assumed by the Crown to the fulfillment of which with the Indians the faith and honour of the Crown is pledged."[13] Although initially written in dissent, this passage was quoted approvingly in 1999 by the majority in *Marshall No 1*.[14] Further examples exist within earlier jurisprudence, such as the 1966 decision *R v George*.[15] In that case, again in dissent, Cartwright J implored his fellow SCC justices to give a broader interpretation to the treaty the accused argued protected him from regulatory prosecution, saying, "We should, I think, endeavour to construe the treaty of 1827 and those Acts of Parliament which bear upon the question before us in such manner that the honour of the Sovereign may be upheld."[16] Determining the source of the doctrine is not as important as recognizing its long-standing, overarching nature.

The contemporary doctrine began to take shape, as mentioned above, in *Guerin*, before being expanded upon in *R v Sparrow*[17] and made explicit in *Badger*. In *Guerin*, the SCC determined that a fiduciary duty arises from the fact that Indigenous Nations in Canada cannot alienate their interests in land to any entity but the Crown; this, the Court said, creates a responsibility on the part of the Crown to deal with surrendered land "for the use and benefit of the surrendering Band."[18] In *Sparrow*, the Court connected the fiduciary duty of *Guerin* to an underlying concept that the Crown must perform its obligations "to a high standard of honourable dealing with respect to the [A]boriginal peoples of Canada."[19] In *Wewaykum Indian Band v Canada*, the SCC imposed limits on the fiduciary duty, saying that it arises only in relation to "specific Indian interests."[20] No such limitation appears to exist for the honour of the Crown. In *Badger*, the SCC made clear that the honour of the Crown inheres to all aspects of the relationship, whether fiduciary, treaty, or otherwise, saying, "The honour of the Crown is always at stake in its dealings with Indian people."[21] Although the SCC in *Manitoba Metis Federation* declared that "not all interactions between the Crown and Aboriginal people engage" the honour of the Crown,[22] the decision provides few examples of these situations, saying merely, "The honour of the Crown will not be engaged by a constitutional obligation in which Aboriginal peoples simply have a strong interest. Nor will it be engaged by a constitutional obligation owed to a group partially composed of Aboriginal peoples."[23] It appears that the honour of the Crown is engaged each time a Crown obligation to an *identifiable* Indigenous group is at issue; in the case of treaties, the honour of the Crown can be presumed to apply because these treaties only exist between the Crown and identifiable Indigenous groups, whether First Nations, groups of Nations, or, in the context of modern treaties, corporations mandated to represent an Indigenous group, such as the Makivvik Corporation, established under the terms of the James Bay and Northern Quebec Agreement to represent the Inuit in Nunavik (northern Quebec).[24]

Whereas *Sparrow* and *Badger* are fishing and hunting regulations cases, *Guerin* is a land-claims case. The doctrine has been applied to subsequent land claims such as *Manitoba Metis Federation*, duty to consult cases such as *Haida Nation v British Columbia (Minister of Forests)*,[25] and even administrative law cases such as *Rio Tinto Alcan v Carrier Sekani Tribal Council*,[26] showing the flexibility and broad applicability of the doctrine.

Because the honour of the Crown inheres to all aspects of the Crown-Indigenous relationship, it can be regarded as a "bedrock" doctrine, from which emerge a variety of related doctrines. But just as a spruce differs from a birch even as they grow from the same ground, these related doctrines have their own characteristics, rules, tests, and limits, not necessarily connected to any characteristics of the honour of the Crown. In fact, the honour of the Crown has been held to give rise to no substantive rights, only procedural rights. As the SCC held in *Manitoba Metis Federation*, the honour of the Crown "is not a cause of action itself; rather, it speaks to *how* obligations that attract it must be fulfilled."[27]

Because it is a procedural right and not a substantive one, a breach of the honour of the Crown is not susceptible to justification under the *Sparrow* test the way other treaty rights are. In *Sparrow* itself, the SCC determined that even when a restriction of an Aboriginal right is justified by furthering a valid legislative objective, any restriction authorized by the test "must uphold the honour of the Crown."[28] Although decided in an Aboriginal rights context, the *Sparrow* test applies to treaty rights via *Badger*, with necessary adjustments for the differing context.[29] These tests will be discussed in detail later in this chapter.

Because the honour of the Crown arises "from the Crown's assertion of sovereignty over an Aboriginal people and *de facto* control of land and resources that were formerly in the control of that people,"[30] it also arises when the assertion of sovereignty occurs.[31] The date of the assertion of sovereignty by the Crown varies across Canada and is often a finding of fact necessary for a trial judge to make. As an example, in Ontario, *Royal Proclamation, 1763* typically serves as the assertion of sovereignty,[32] whereas in British Columbia — where colonization began somewhat later — the assertion of sovereignty has been tied to the Treaty Between Her Majesty and the United States of America, for the Settlement of the Oregon Boundary, concluded in 1846.[33] It appears necessary for a trial judge to identify an instance of sovereignty, whether proclamation, treaty, or otherwise, in which to ground the assertion of sovereignty.

Like many other aspects of Aboriginal and treaty jurisprudence, the SCC has concluded that a generous interpretation of the meaning of honourable conduct is necessary. As the SCC explained in *Haida Nation*:

> The honour of the Crown is always at stake in its dealings with Aboriginal peoples . . . . It is not a mere incantation, but rather a core precept that finds its application in concrete practices.
>
> The historical roots of the principle of the honour of the Crown suggest that it must be understood generously in order to reflect the underlying realities from which it stems. In all its dealings with Aboriginal peoples, from the assertion of sovereignty to the resolution of claims and the implementation of treaties, the Crown must act honourably. Nothing less is required if we are to achieve "the reconciliation of the pre-existence of [A]boriginal societies with the sovereignty of the Crown."[34]

The SCC has commented that the essence of honourable conduct is keeping promises that are made: "[I]f the honour of the Crown is pledged to the fulfillment of its obligations, it follows then that the honour of the Crown requires the Crown to endeavour to ensure its obligations are fulfilled."[35] That being said, the SCC has also written that "what constitutes honourable conduct will vary with the circumstances," and "the duty that flows from the honour of the Crown varies with the situation in which it is engaged."[36] In *Manitoba Metis Federation*, the SCC identified four situations in which the doctrine has previously been applied, although it is important to keep in mind, as Dickson J suggested in *Guerin*, that these categories, "like those of negligence, should not be considered closed."[37] These four doctrines are: the duty to negotiate treaties honourably and avoid the appearance of sharp dealing; the fiduciary duty; the related duties to consult and accommodate; and the duty to diligently and purposively fulfill Crown obligations.[38] The duty to negotiate honourably is related to treaty formation and is discussed in Chapter 1. The other three doctrines are discussed below.

The Fiduciary Duty

The existence of a fiduciary relationship between the Crown and Indigenous peoples in Canada was first determined in *Guerin*.[39] Per *Manitoba Metis Federation*, two types of fiduciary relationships are possible within the Crown-Indigenous relationship. The first, known as the ad hoc duty, arises in the same way as it might between the Crown and any person or group of peoples: via an undertaking. The ad hoc fiduciary duty is not restricted to the Indigenous context. The ad hoc duty arises when the following conditions are met:

1. An undertaking by the alleged fiduciary to act in the best interests of the alleged beneficiary or beneficiaries;
2. A defined person or class of persons vulnerable to a fiduciary's control (the beneficiary or beneficiaries); and
3. A legal or substantial practical interest of the beneficiary or beneficiaries that stands to be adversely affected by the alleged fiduciary's exercise of discretion or control.

This type of undertaking is incredibly rare between the Crown and any segment of society and, even in the Indigenous context, is governed entirely by the well-established rules of equity.[40] For this reason, this treatise focuses exclusively on the type of fiduciary duty unique to the Crown-Indigenous relationship, the aptly named *sui generis* duty.

The *sui generis* duty arises, per *Wewaykum* and *Haida Nation*, where

1. The Crown undertakes a discretionary control over
2. A specific or cognizable Aboriginal interest.[41]

In determining whether the *sui generis* duty has arisen on the facts, the SCC focused on the definitions of "discretionary control" and "Aboriginal interest." Discretionary control is, per *Guerin*, connected to the potential for harm caused by one party that cannot be mitigated by the other. In that decision, Dickson J quoted Professor Ernest Weinrib, who wrote that "the hallmark of a fiduciary relation is that the relative legal positions are such that one party is *at the mercy* of the other's discretion."[42] Justice Dickson appeared to broaden this definition slightly in order to encompass situations that present less potential for risk and focused more on the duty to provide a benefit when he wrote:

> Where by statute, by agreement or perhaps by unilateral undertaking one party has an obligation to act for the benefit of another, and that obligation carries with it a discretionary power, the party thus empowered becomes a fiduciary.[43]

Although the question of discretionary control may be an important one in a case about Aboriginal rights, in a treaty rights context, the treaty itself — especially a land-cession treaty — leads to a presumption that the first part of the test is fulfilled. In such a context, as per *Guerin*, by *agreement*, the Crown has taken on the *obligation* to act in the best interests of the Nation or Nations from which the surrender of territory is taken, and the use to which the Crown puts the newly acquired land is within its *discretionary power*. But even in the peace and alliance era, subsequent events have given rise to the level of discretionary control necessary to ground a fiduciary duty. In *Marshall No 1*, the SCC pointed to the relationship between the treaty right to fish and the Crown's discretionary control over fishing regulations and licensing to ground a *sui generis* fiduciary duty.[44]

Outside of the treaty context, the concept of a "specific or cognizable Aboriginal interest" may be the question on which a case turns. In *Manitoba Metis Federation*, for example, the Metis practice of holding land individually was deemed "not sufficient to establish an *Aboriginal* interest in land" because the SCC defined an Aboriginal interest in land as "communal."[45] In a treaty context, the Aboriginal nature of the interest can be presumed, absent extraordinary facts. This is because the Crown only concluded treaties with First Nations, ensuring that there is no question that the rights that arise out of treaty are Aboriginal interests. If extraordinary facts create doubt about the nature of an interest, the "integral to a distinctive culture" test, or *Van der Peet* test, will determine the existence of a specific or cognizable Aboriginal interest. Although significant nuance is added by Lamer CJ in his decision, the outlines of the test are below:

1. Courts must take into account the perspective of Aboriginal peoples themselves.

2. Courts must identify precisely the nature of the claim being made in determining whether an Aboriginal claimant has demonstrated the existence of an Aboriginal right.

3. In order to be integral, a practice, custom, or tradition must be of central significance to the Aboriginal society in question.

4. The practices, customs, and traditions that constitute Aboriginal rights are those that have continuity with the practices, customs, and traditions that existed prior to contact.

5. Courts must approach the rules of evidence in light of the evidentiary difficulties inherent in adjudicating Aboriginal claims.

6. Claims to Aboriginal rights must be adjudicated on a specific rather than general basis.

7. For a practice, custom, or tradition to constitute an Aboriginal right, it must be of independent significance to the Aboriginal culture in which it exists.

8. The integral to a distinctive culture test requires that a practice, custom, or tradition be distinctive; it does not require that that practice, custom, or tradition be distinct.

9. The influence of European culture will only be relevant to the inquiry if it is demonstrated that the practice, custom, or tradition is only integral because of that influence.

10. Courts must take into account both the relationship of Aboriginal Peoples to the land and the distinctive societies and cultures of Aboriginal Peoples.[46]

Although no historical treaties exist between the Crown and the Metis Nation, should the parties see fit to conclude a modern treaty, the test for a specific and cognizable Aboriginal interest within the context of the Metis would be the *Van der Peet* test as modified by the decision in *R v Powley*. In that case, the SCC acknowledged that because the integral to a distinctive culture test was based on pre-contact practices, it would be inappropriate to apply the same test to the Metis, a Nation born of contact.[47]

As the SCC stated in *Wewaykum*, "The content of the Crown's fiduciary duty towards [A]boriginal peoples varies with the nature and importance of the interest sought to be protected,"[48] and "even in the traditional trust context not all obligations existing between the parties to a well-recognized fiduciary relationship are themselves fiduciary in nature."[49] This makes it difficult to say, objectively, what the content of the fiduciary duty is; instead, both the existence of the duty and the content of the duty stemming from the nature of the relationship and demands of the situation are findings of fact for the trial judge. At minimum, however, the jurisprudence appears to demand "loyalty, good faith, full disclosure appropriate to the subject matter and with 'ordinary' diligence in what it reasonably regarded as the best interest of the beneficiaries" at all times.[50] This is a low bar: note the demand of "loyalty" but not the "utmost loyalty" that would be demanded of an ad hoc fiduciary.[51] Similarly, "good faith" is not the equivalent of the *uberrimae fidei*, or "utmost good faith" demanded of an ad hoc fiduciary.[52] Finally, phrases such as "appropriate to the subject matter" and "reasonably regarded" give significant discretion to a fiduciary to define their own duties and execute them according to subjective standards. The lack of clear standards makes it difficult for equity to "supervise the relationship" in order to hold fiduciaries to the "strict standard of conduct" promised in *Guerin*.[53]

Where the fiduciary duty has been found to apply and the case revolves around reserve land, the SCC has identified an objective change to the content of the fiduciary duty demanded by the changed context. As the Court wrote in *Wewaykum*, "Once a reserve is created, the content of the Crown's fiduciary duty expands to include the protection and preservation of the band's quasi-proprietary interest in the reserve from exploitation," including "exploitation by the Crown itself."[54]

The effect of this expansion was considered in *Southwind v Canada*. In that case, a portion of a reserve was taken for a purpose necessary to the public interest: the building of a hydroelectric reservoir.[55] The taking was unlawful because not only was there no legal expropriation, the taking did not accord with the terms of Treaty No. 3 for the taking up of reserve land.[56] At trial, the plaintiffs were awarded compensation based on a calculation of the value of the land when it was taken in 1929, which is consistent with general expropriation principles.[57] On appeal to the SCC, the Court ruled that the fiduciary duty, as applied to the quasi-proprietary interest in reserve land, demanded significantly greater protection by the fiduciary to the First Nation beneficiaries. The SCC commented: "By looking solely at the amount the [Lac Seul First Nation] would have received if Canada had complied with the general law relating to expropriation, the trial judge gave no effect to the unique obligations imposed by the fiduciary duty."[58] To comply with the standard of a fiduciary over reserve land, equitable compensation needed to consider highest and best use with the benefit of hindsight, which meant that — unlike in a typical expropriation — the actual value of the land to the hydroelectricity project was to be the basis upon which the value of compensation was determined.[59] The requirement to preserve and protect reserve land under the expanded fiduciary duty demanded significantly higher compensation when the duty had been violated.

Questions have arisen about the content of the fiduciary duty when a reserve is *promised* but never delivered. In *Williams Lake Indian Band v. Canada (Aboriginal Affairs and Northern Development)*, the SCC had to consider the Crown's fiduciary duty in light of the relationship between the Crown in right of British Columbia and the Crown in right of Canada as British Columbia entered Confederation. Although British Columbia was still a British colony, settlers began to move into unsurveyed lands in the Williams Lake area, displacing Indigenous inhabitants.[60] In 1860, the colony enacted a proclamation that stated that such lands were not available for pre-emption by settlers but took no steps to mark out such lands or create a reserve.[61] When British Columbia entered Confederation in 1871, Canada took over responsibility for reserve creation.[62] The federal Crown acknowledged that allowing settlers to pre-empt the traditional territory of the Williams Lake Band had been a mistake but refused to interfere with settlers' rights in the area.[63]

The SCC ruled that such conduct gave rise to a "cognizable" Aboriginal interest in the land even before the finalization of a reserve, a precondition of the fiduciary duty.[64] The other precondition, discretionary control, was fulfilled by the federal Crown's taking responsibility for reserve creation under the *British Columbia Terms of Union*.[65] However, without the quasi-proprietary interest in land that arises following the creation of a reserve, the Crown owed merely the minimum content of the *sui generis* duty as identified in *Wewaykum*, not the expanded version that was considered in *Southwind*. The SCC justified its decision in this way:

> The circumstances in which a fiduciary obligation arises shape its content.... The content of the Crown's *sui generis* fiduciary duty varies to take into account its broader public obligations.... Prior to the acquisition of a "legal interest" in land that is subject to the reserve creation process, the Crown's *sui generis* fiduciary duty is "to act with respect to the interest of the [A]boriginal peoples with loyalty, good faith, full disclosure appropriate to the subject matter and with 'ordinary' diligence in what it reasonably regard[s] as the best interest of the beneficiaries".... In such circumstances, though, the Crown's fiduciary duty is limited by its obligation to "have regard to the interest of all affected parties" and to be even-handed among competing beneficiaries.... Fulfilling this flexible equitable obligation entails consideration of the nature and importance of the beneficiary's interest and competing interests; although the Crown cannot ignore the reality of conflicting demands, neither does the existence of such demands absolve it altogether of its fiduciary duty in its efforts to reconcile them fairly.[66]

This determination raises one final aspect of the *sui generis* fiduciary duty: it is susceptible to a balancing of rights between Indigenous peoples and citizens of Canada. The balancing process is the site where the difference between the loyalty demanded of a *sui generis* fiduciary and the "utmost" loyalty of the typical duty begin to clash. In any normal fiduciary duty, no balancing is possible because the fiduciary must put the beneficiary's interests above those of anyone else.

Balancing rights within the context of the Crown's fiduciary obligations to Indigenous peoples in Canada is a case-specific exercise.[67] Where a fiduciary duty is found to exist in relation to a cognizable Aboriginal interest, Indigenous peoples are owed some level of priority over the interest, although not exclusivity, and balancing this priority interest over other interests falls to the Crown. The Crown is expected to balance these competing interests at a standard of reasonableness, in a process the SCC has compared to the *Oakes* test:

Under the minimal impairment branch of the *Oakes* test ..., where the government is balancing the interests of competing groups, the court does not scrutinize the government's actions so as to determine whether the government took the least rights-impairing action possible; instead the court considers the reasonableness of the government's actions, taking into account the need to assess "conflicting scientific evidence and differing justified demands on scarce resources." ... [Where the government balances Aboriginal rights against the larger society's,] courts should assess the government's actions not to see whether the government has given exclusivity to that right (the least drastic means) but rather to determine whether the government has taken into account the existence and importance of such rights.[68]

Ultimately, when undertaking the balancing among legal rights required by the *sui generis* fiduciary duty, the Crown's duty is "to reconcile those interests fairly."[69] The questions of justification and the propriety of importing an *Oakes* analysis into Aboriginal law will be explored in the next section: Restricting and Regulating Treaty Rights.

The Duty to Consult

Although it most typically arises where Aboriginal rights are in question and not in a treaty context,[70] the duty to consult, stemming from the honour of the Crown, has been held to apply to both historical treaties[71] and modern ones.[72] The jurisprudence that applies in the Aboriginal rights context applies equally in the treaty rights context, although, in the treaty rights context, determining whether the duty arises is significantly easier.

According to *Haida Nation*, an Aboriginal rights case where the duty to consult was first determined, the duty arises where "the Crown has knowledge, real or constructive, of the potential existence of the Aboriginal right or title and contemplates conduct that might adversely affect it."[73] In *Rio Tinto Alcan*, another Aboriginal rights case, this test was broken down into three constituent elements: "(1) the Crown's knowledge, actual or constructive, of a potential Aboriginal claim or right; (2) contemplated Crown conduct; and (3) the potential that the contemplated conduct may adversely affect an Aboriginal claim or right."[74] Later in the same decision, the SCC discussed the effect of a treaty on the first element, stating that where a treaty exists, Crown knowledge can essentially be presumed:

> The threshold, informed by the need to maintain the honour of the Crown, is not high. Actual knowledge arises when a claim has been filed in court or advanced in the context of negotiations, or when a treaty right may be impacted.[75]

As for the second element, contemplated Crown conduct, again the threshold is low. In *Rio Tinto Alcan*, the SCC determined that any "conduct that *may* adversely impact on the claim or right in question" will satisfy this element.[76] The exercise of statutory powers will trigger the duty, as will "strategic, higher level decisions" such as land management planning, resource extraction planning or reviews, inquiries into infrastructure, and other inquiries.[77] In *Mikisew Cree First Nation v Canada (Governor General in Council)*, the SCC determined that the duty to consult does not arise in the context of legislative decision making, based on the need to maintain a clear separation of powers.[78] A concurrence by Abella J, which agreed with the result based on a jurisdictional issue but dissented on the issue of whether the duty to consult could arise via legislative decision making, insisted that the concept of the honour of the Crown demanded a conclusion that all Crown decision making be subject to the doctrines that ensure that the Crown conducts itself with honour, writing:

> The duty to consult arises based on the effect, not the source, of the government action. The Crown's overarching responsibility to act honourably in all its dealings with Indigenous peoples does not depend on the formal label applied to the type of action that the government takes with respect to Aboriginal rights and interests protected by s. 35 of the *Constitution Act, 1982*. As a constitutional imperative, the honour of the Crown cannot be undermined, let alone extinguished, by the legislature's assertion of parliamentary sovereignty.[79]

Given the "generous, purposive approach"[80] the SCC has taken to the duty to consult and the fact that Crown conduct need merely be "contemplated" according to the test — not to mention that the Crown's honour hangs in the balance — it stands to reason that any government decision making, including legislative, ought to trigger the second element, as Abella J suggests, especially in the treaty context. Treaty rights are protected by section 35 of the *Constitution Act, 1982*, and, via section 52 of the same Act, "any law that is inconsistent with the provisions of the Constitution is, to the extent of the inconsistency, of no force or effect."[81] In that context, a refusal by the legislative branch to comply with the doctrines that arise out of the treaty relationship, such as the honour of the Crown or the duty to consult, fails to accord with the Constitution.

The third element likely provides the most challenging threshold to a claimant, but, again, it is not particularly high. As the SCC wrote in *Rio Tinto Alcan*, "The claimant must show a causal relationship between the proposed government conduct or decision and a potential for adverse impacts on pending Aboriginal claims or rights."[82] The jurisprudence demands a mere "causal relationship," not "but for" causation, and demands only the "potential" for an adverse impact. This is in keeping with the "generous, purposive approach" to the doctrine, which exists because "the doctrine's purpose ... is 'to recognize that actions affecting unproven Aboriginal title or rights or treaty rights can have irreversible effects that are not in keeping with the honour of the Crown.'"[83] In fact, indirect or long-term causation will suffice. As the SCC allowed:

[A]s discussed in connection with what constitutes Crown conduct, high-level management decisions or structural changes to the resource's management may also adversely affect Aboriginal claims or rights even if these decisions have no "immediate impact on lands and resources" .... This is because such structural changes to the resources management may set the stage for further decisions that will have a *direct* adverse impact on land and resources.[84]

If the duty to consult arises on the test from *Haida Nation*, the Court's next step is to determine the content of the duty in the context of the contemplated Crown conduct. In *Haida Nation* itself, the SCC characterized this process as one of placing the content of the duty along a "spectrum" based on the strength of the Indigenous Nation's claim. The Court discussed the lower end of the spectrum and its requisite duties in this fashion:

> At one end of the spectrum lie cases where the claim to title is weak, the Aboriginal right limited, or the potential for infringement minor. In such cases, the only duty on the Crown may be to give notice, disclose information, and discuss any issues raised in response to the notice.[85]

The SCC then discussed what may be necessary when the duty to consult arises at the higher end of the spectrum:

> At the other end of the spectrum lie cases where a strong *prima facie* case for the claim is established, the right and potential infringement is of high significance to the Aboriginal peoples, and the risk of non-compensable damage is high. In such cases deep consultation, aimed at finding a satisfactory interim solution, may be required. While precise requirements will vary with the circumstances, the consultation required at this stage may entail the opportunity to make submissions for consideration, formal participation in the decision-making process, and provision of written reasons to show that Aboriginal concerns were considered and to reveal the impact they had on the decision. This list is neither exhaustive, nor mandatory for every case.[86]

It can be challenging to actualize this aspect of the doctrine because, as the SCC reminded us in *Haida Nation*, "[e]very case must be approached individually."[87] Ultimately, the content of the duty to consult is determined by identifying "what is required to maintain the honour of the Crown and to effect reconciliation between the Crown and the Aboriginal peoples with respect to the interests at stake."[88]

This treatise suggests that where a treaty defines the Crown-Indigenous relationship, the duty to consult should be presumed at the high end of the spectrum. The "interests at stake" are codified within the solemn promise of the treaty — no prima facie case is necessary — and the existence of the negotiated instrument shows that the infringement of the rights it contains is presumably of "high significance" to the Indigenous signatories; otherwise, they never would have formed part of the agreement in the first place.

The assertion made in the paragraph above does not find direct jurisprudential support. In *Mikisew Cree* — one of the few duty to consult decisions in a treaty context — Canada planned to build a winter road through the Mikisew Reserve in Treaty No. 8 territory without consulting their treaty partners. Although the Crown had the right to "take up" land for public purposes under the treaty, the SCC ruled that such a right is "subject to its duty to consult and, if appropriate, accommodate First Nations' interests before reducing the area over which their members may continue to pursue their hunting, trapping and fishing rights."[89] When the Crown determined where on the spectrum the duty of consultation fell, however, the SCC wrote this:

> In this case, given that the Crown is proposing to build a fairly minor winter road on *surrendered* lands where the Mikisew hunting, fishing and trapping rights are expressly subject to the "taking up" limitation, ... the Crown's duty lies at the lower end of the spectrum.[90]

The determination that the duty to consult lies at the lower end of the spectrum is undercut, however, by the SCC's description of the content of the duty in this case:

> The Crown was required to provide notice to the Mikisew and to engage directly with them (and not, as seems to have been the case here, as an afterthought to a general public consultation with Park users). This engagement ought to have included the provision of information about the project addressing what the Crown knew to be Mikisew interests and what the Crown anticipated might be the potential adverse impact on those interests. *The Crown was required to solicit and to listen carefully to the Mikisew concerns, and to attempt to minimize adverse impacts on the Mikisew hunting, fishing and trapping rights.*[91]

Compare this description of the content of the duty at the "lower end" of the spectrum with the content of the duty at the high end of the spectrum in *Haida Nation*:

> In such cases deep consultation, aimed at finding a satisfactory interim solution, may be required. While precise requirements will vary with the circumstances, the consultation required at this stage

may entail the opportunity to make submissions for consideration, formal participation in the decision-making process, and provision of written reasons to show that Aboriginal concerns were considered and to reveal the impact they had on the decision.[92]

There are clear similarities between the content of each duty that cannot simply be explained by taking an individual approach, as dictated by *Haida Nation* itself.[93] This treatise suggests that there is little difference between concepts such as "a satisfactory interim solution" and an "attempt to minimize adverse impacts" on treaty rights; similarly, there is little difference between "the opportunity to make submissions for consideration [and] formal participation in the decision-making process" in *Haida Nation* and the requirement in *Mikisew Cree* to "engage directly" in a specific consultation and "to solicit and to listen carefully to the Mikisew concerns" about the proposal. In *Haida Nation*, the SCC described the content of the duty to consult at the lower end of the spectrum as encompassing duties to "give notice, disclose information, and discuss any issues raised in response to the notice."[94] Despite the SCC's determination that the duty to consult in *Mikisew Cree* was at the lower end of the spectrum, by determining the content of the duty as it did, the SCC appears to have acknowledged that, in reality, the duty was at the higher end.

It should be noted that responsibilities within the duty to accommodate analysis do not fall solely on the Crown. Although the duty itself always remains with and must be fulfilled by the Crown, the procedural aspects of fulfilling the duty can be delegated to third parties. As the SCC wrote in *Haida Nation*:

> [T]he duty to consult and accommodate, as discussed above, flows from the Crown's assumption of sovereignty over lands and resources formerly held by the Aboriginal group. This theory provides no support for an obligation on third parties to consult or accommodate. The Crown alone remains legally responsible for the consequences of its actions and interactions with third parties, that affect Aboriginal interests. The Crown may delegate procedural aspects of consultation to industry proponents seeking a particular development; this is not infrequently done in environmental assessments. . . . However,

the ultimate legal responsibility for consultation and accommodation rests with the Crown. The honour of the Crown cannot be delegated.[95]

In the same decision, the SCC also clarified that the duty is not borne solely by the *federal* Crown; provinces, as representatives of the Crown, have duties to Indigenous peoples as well. Whereas in *Haida Nation* the Crown in right of British Columbia argued that provincial rights to "Lands, Mines, Minerals and Royalties" outlined in section 109 of the *Constitution Act, 1867*[96] were exclusive and could not be limited by section 35 of the *Constitution Act, 1982*'s protection of Aboriginal and treaty rights, the SCC relied on *Delgamuukw v British Columbia* to determine that, under section 109, provinces took their rights subject to prior interests, which included Indigenous interests.[97] It appears that, because the duty to consult arises from the honour of the Crown and because the honour of the Crown arises "from the Crown's assertion of sovereignty over an Aboriginal people and *de facto* control of land and resources that were formerly in the control of that people,"[98] the provincial Crown's *de facto* control of land and resources creates a provincial duty to accommodate on the same three-part test in *Haida Nation* and *Rio Tinto Alcan*.[99]

The Duty to Accommodate

The duty to accommodate stems directly from the duty to consult, although not every consultation will lead to a duty to accommodate. As the SCC wrote in *Haida Nation*, the need to accommodate an Indigenous group in regard to Crown decision making cannot be identified until the consultation process does so:

> When the consultation process suggests amendment of Crown policy, we arrive at the stage of accommodation. *Thus the effect of good faith consultation may be to reveal a duty to accommodate.* Where a strong *prima facie* case exists for the claim, and the consequences of the government's proposed decision may adversely affect it in a significant way, addressing the Aboriginal concerns may require taking steps to avoid irreparable harm or to minimize the effects of infringement, pending final resolution of the underlying claim.[100]

Little jurisprudence exists regarding the duty to accommodate, and its content is difficult to discern because of this. This should come as no surprise as in *Haida Nation* — the case that first identified the duty — the SCC left significant discretion in the hands of the trial judge to determine whether the duty to accommodate arises on the facts but offered little direction. Rather than clear steps or minimum content, the SCC said that addressing Indigenous concerns may require taking steps to accommodate; whether those steps are necessary and how far those steps need go remain something of a mystery.

One clearly necessary aspect, however, is good faith. As the SCC made clear, good faith is not solely a Crown responsibility but one shared by Indigenous peoples as well. The Court also made clear that hard bargaining does not negate good faith:

> At all stages, good faith on both sides is required. The common thread on the Crown's part must be "the intention of substantially addressing [Aboriginal] concerns" as they are raised ... , through a meaningful process of consultation. Sharp dealing is not permitted. However, there is no duty to agree; rather, the commitment is to a meaningful process of consultation. As for Aboriginal claimants, they must not frustrate the Crown's reasonable good faith attempts, nor should they take unreasonable positions to thwart government from making decisions or acting in cases where, despite meaningful consultation, agreement is not reached .... Mere hard bargaining, however, will not offend an Aboriginal people's right to be consulted.[101]

With the power differential between the Crown and Indigenous Nations in Canada being what it is, however, good faith should be considered most important — and bad faith guarded against more vigilantly — for the Crown. After all, Crown decision making — or contemplated decision making — creates the parameters from which the duty to consult and accommodate is determined. The Crown has immense power within this paradigm. Using bad faith, it could turn these parameters into a poison pill by introducing multiple elements it knows will prove unacceptable to an Indigenous Nation. By removing only one of these elements — while leaving the rest — the Crown can argue that it has meaningfully accommodated the concerns of its

Indigenous partners, thus fulfilling its duty. Indigenous Nations have no similar powers. Determining whether consultation and accommodation have occurred in good faith in a situation akin to the above hypothetical is difficult, justifying a higher level of scrutiny.

By no means is this meant to imply that Indigenous Nations cannot act in bad faith. In *Ktunaxa Nation v British Columbia (Forests, Lands and Natural Resource Operations)*, an Aboriginal rights case but applicable to the duty to consult and accommodate in the treaty rights context, Ktunaxa Nation sought to block the development of a ski resort in a part of the Nation's traditional territory called Qat'muk by judicially reviewing the decision of the minister of forests, lands, and natural resource operations to approve the development. Qat'muk is a place of "spiritual significance" to the Nation, home to both "an important population of grizzly bears and to Grizzly Bear Spirit, or Kławła Tukłułak?is," which the SCC describes as a principal aspect of Ktunaxa religion and cosmology.[102] The development of a permanent ski resort, the Ktunaxa said, "would drive Grizzly Bear Spirit from Qat'muk and irrevocably impair their religious beliefs and practices."[103] The SCC described the consultations to that point and the positions of the parties in the following way:

> Negotiations spanning two decades and deep consultation had taken place. Many changes had been made to the project to accommodate the Ktunaxa's spiritual claims. At a point when it appeared all major issues had been resolved, the Ktunaxa, in the form of the Late-2009 Claim, adopted a new, absolute position that no accommodation was possible because permanent structures would drive Grizzly Bear Spirit from Qat'muk. The Minister sought to consult with the Ktunaxa on the newly formulated claim, but was told that there was no point in further consultation given the new Ktunaxa position that no accommodation was possible and that only total rejection of the project would satisfy them.[104]

Because the consultation had spanned over two decades and had resulted in prior accommodations, and the Ktunaxa had taken an uncompromising position, the SCC found that the minister's conclusion that the duty to consult and accommodate had been fulfilled and the decision to approve the development was reasonable.[105]

Ktunaxa Nation demands an extremely high standard of consultation and accommodation before these twin duties can be said to have been fulfilled. It should be noted, however, that the context of *Ktunaxa Nation* was an "as-yet unproven" Aboriginal rights claim.[106] Where a proven treaty right is at issue, it is reasonable to assume that the duty to consult and accommodate could demand an even higher standard than that described above.

The Duty to Diligently and Purposively Fulfill Crown Obligations

The duty to diligently and purposively fulfill Crown obligations to Indigenous peoples stems from an assumption in treaty interpretation that "the Crown intends to fulfil its promises."[107] The SCC reiterated this assumption in *Mikisew Cree* and connected it to the honour of the Crown, writing, "[T]he honour of the Crown was pledged to the fulfilment of its obligations to the Indians" and further remarking that this policy is long-standing, going "as far back as the *Royal Proclamation of 1763.*"[108] In *Manitoba Metis Federation*, the SCC took this assumption one step further, writing that "if the honour of the Crown is pledged to the fulfillment of its obligations, it follows then that the honour of the Crown requires the Crown to endeavour to ensure its obligations are fulfilled."[109]

The Court also made clear in the same decision that this duty of purposive and diligent fulfillment applies not only to historical treaties but to modern treaties as well, citing the James Bay and Northern Quebec Agreement and the determination in *Quebec (Attorney General) v Moses* that the parties to the agreement are expected to "carry out their work with due diligence."[110]

According to the SCC, there are two aspects of the duty, which work in a particular order: the first is the purposive interpretation, and the second is the diligent fulfillment.[111] Purposive interpretation is a long-standing aspect of treaty interpretation. In *Manitoba Metis Federation*, the Court determined that such an interpretation "cannot be a legalistic one that divorces the words from their purpose."[112] In *Marshall*

No 1, criticizing the lower courts for taking a narrow interpretation of a trade clause in a peace and friendship treaty, Binnie J wrote:

> I do not think an interpretation of events that turns a positive Mi'kmaq trade demand into a negative Mi'kmaq covenant is consistent with the honour and integrity of the Crown. . . . The trade arrangement must be interpreted in a manner which gives meaning and substance to the promises made by the Crown. In my view, with respect, the interpretation adopted by the courts below left the Mi'kmaq with an empty shell of a treaty promise.[113]

Justice Binnie further connected the requirement for purposive interpretation to the long-standing treaty interpretation principle that ambiguity in a treaty document must be resolved in favour of its Indigenous signatories, a principle that emerges from *Badger*, *Sparrow*, and *R v White*, among others.[114]

Once an interpretation that gives meaning and substance to the Crown promise has been arrived at, the court asks whether it has been diligently fulfilled. Diligent fulfillment is connected to the purpose behind the promise, the SCC said, writing, "To fulfill this duty, Crown servants must seek to perform the obligation in a way that pursues the purpose behind the promise."[115] In *Saugeen First Nation v The Attorney General of Canada*, which determined that a promise to protect the Bruce Peninsula "from the encroachment of the whites" for two Anishinaabe First Nations in Treaty No. 45½ was breached, Matheson J approached this aspect of the test by asking, "What did the Crown do to diligently fulfill the treaty obligation to protect the Peninsula, and was it enough?"[116] It is likely to be a rare case where the Crown has made a treaty promise and done absolutely nothing to fulfill it, so the question "was it enough?" appears to be the most important aspect of the test.

In *Saugeen First Nation*, the issue was squatting by settlers on the Bruce Peninsula, something the First Nations argued should have been addressed by the Crown based on the treaty promise. And, as Matheson J determined, the Crown did address it to some extent; she noted that the "Crown took general steps (such as passing legislation) and reactive steps (in response to complaints)" to combat the issue but concluded that "the circumstances required more."[117] Despite some efforts by the Crown, it knew that squatting had continued and had, in fact, worsened. When the efforts to curb squatting did not fulfill the purpose of the promise, Matheson J found that "more proactive steps, focused on the Peninsula, were needed" to avoid breaching the treaty.[118]

This does not mean, however, that the Crown must fulfill the purpose of the promise. *Manitoba Metis Federation* allows for significant Crown discretion within the context of the test. The test does not demand that the promise was fulfilled, only that "the Crown act with diligence to *pursue* the fulfillment of the purposes of the obligation."[119] Harkening back to the idea that the Crown intends to fulfill its promises while privileging the idea of intention over achievement, the SCC wrote:

> Not every mistake or negligent act in implementing a constitutional obligation to an Aboriginal people brings dishonour to the Crown. Implementation, in the way of human affairs, may be imperfect. However, a persistent pattern of errors and indifference that substantially frustrates the purposes of a solemn promise may amount to a betrayal of the Crown's duty to act honourably in fulfilling its promise. Nor does the honour of the Crown constitute a guarantee that the purposes of the promise will be achieved, as circumstances and events may prevent fulfillment, despite the Crown's diligent efforts.[120]

Therefore, the question is not whether the promise was fulfilled but whether the Crown's *pursuit* of fulfillment was diligent enough.

Restricting and Regulating Treaty Rights: The *Badger* Test

As first mentioned in Chapter 1, treaty rights are not limitless: they can be regulated and restricted by the Canadian government if such regulations or restrictions can be justified. It may seem somewhat more than curious, perhaps even unfair, that treaty agreements — which this treatise defines as *international* agreements, although not necessarily *interstate* agreements — could be regulated or restricted unilaterally as long as such regulations are justifiable under the aegis of that side's justice system. But, in *Badger*, Cory J determined that the text of Treaty

No. 8, coupled with the existence of conservation laws made prior to its signing, meant that "the Indians would have understood that, by the terms of the Treaty, the government would be permitted to pass regulations with respect to conservation."[121] Thus, it appears that shared expectations — a contractual principle — justifies unilateral restriction.

Many elements of the *Badger* test must be understood through the facts of *Badger* itself, although these elements have been extended and made applicable to situations that do not resemble the factual matrix of *Badger*. In *Badger*, three Cree men with status under Treaty No. 8 were summarily convicted of hunting out of season on privately owned land. On appeal, the men argued that their right to hunt as they did was protected by the treaty, the relevant portion of which read:

> And Her Majesty the Queen HEREBY AGREES with the said Indians that they shall have right to pursue their usual vocations of hunting, trapping and fishing throughout the tract surrendered as heretofore described, subject to such regulations as may from time to time be made by the Government of the country, acting under the authority of Her Majesty, and saving and excepting such tracts as may be required or taken up from time to time for settlement, mining, lumbering, trading or other purposes.[122]

The Crown argued that subsequent legislation, the Natural Resources Transfer Agreement (NRTA), extinguished the right to hunt as explicated in the treaty, such that the right to hunt under Treaty No. 8 was merely what was now allowable as regulated by the NRTA. The SCC set itself the task of determining when and how a treaty right is lawfully regulated. An infringement and justification analysis had recently been determined in an Aboriginal rights context in *Sparrow*, and the Court applied the same principles to a treaty rights context, settling on a four-stage test.[123] The test was expanded to some degree in *Mikisew Cree* when a duty to consult analysis was interjected between the third and fourth stages.[124] Ultimately, the *Badger* test for restricting and regulating treaty rights has five stages:

1. Interpretation of the treaty right
2. Test for extinguishment

3. Test for infringement
4. Duty to consult analysis
5. Justification

These stages of the test will be explored, in turn, below.

Interpretation of the Treaty Right

First, the court must determine what the treaty right at issue is — what activity or practice is being protected by the treaty. This stage utilizes the same nine principles of treaty interpretation discussed in Chapter 2:

1. Aboriginal treaties constitute a unique type of agreement and attract special principles of interpretation ....

2. Treaties should be liberally construed and ambiguities or doubtful expressions should be resolved in favour of the [A]boriginal signatories ....

3. The goal of treaty interpretation is to choose from among the various possible interpretations of common intention the one which best reconciles the interests of both parties at the time the treaty was signed ....

4. In searching for the common intention of the parties, the integrity and honour of the Crown is presumed ....

5. In determining the signatories' respective understanding and intentions, the court must be sensitive to the unique cultural and linguistic differences between the parties ....

6. The words of the treaty must be given the sense which they would naturally have held for the parties at the time ....

7. A technical or contractual interpretation of treaty wording should be avoided ....

8. While construing the language generously, courts cannot alter the terms of the treaty by exceeding what "is possible on the language" or realistic ....

9. Treaty rights of [A]boriginal peoples must not be interpreted in a static or rigid way. They are not frozen at the date of signature. The interpreting court must update treaty rights to provide for their modern exercise. This involves determining what modern

practices are reasonably incidental to the core treaty right in its modern context.[125]

See Chapter 2 for a detailed explanation of each of these principles. In *Badger* itself, the SCC did not need to spend much time interpreting the right in question as an earlier case — *R v Horsemen* — had determined that the right protected by Treaty No. 8 was the right to hunt for food, although not the right to a commercial hunt.[126]

Test for Extinguishment

Second, the court must determine whether the right protected by the treaty has been previously extinguished. This aspect of the *Badger* test stems directly from *Sparrow*. The onus is on the Crown to show on a balance of probabilities that a treaty right has been extinguished, and the test for determining extinguishment is "that the sovereign's intention must be *clear and plain* if it is to extinguish an [A]boriginal right," as in *Sparrow*,[127] or a treaty right, as in *Badger*.[128]

In *Badger*, the question was whether the NRTA showed such a clear and plain intention to extinguish and replace the right to hunt for food. The Court determined that it did not. It looked to the Act as well as the jurisprudence to conclude that the NRTA circumscribed the right "with respect to both the geographical area within which this right may be exercised as well as the regulations which may properly be imposed by the government" but did not extinguish it.[129] Regulation is not the equivalent of extinguishment.

With the treaty right determined to still be in force, the Court turned to the next stage, the infringement analysis.

Test for Infringement

Third, the court must determine whether the impugned conduct actually infringes the right protected. Again, this aspect of the *Badger* test comes directly from *Sparrow*. In *Sparrow*, to determine whether an Aboriginal right had been infringed, the Court dictated three questions and highlighted which party bears the onus for proving an infringement:

First, is the limitation unreasonable? Second, does the regulation impose undue hardship? Third, does the regulation deny to the holders of the right their preferred means of exercising that right? The onus of proving a *prima facie* infringement lies on the individual or group challenging the legislation.[130]

Badger makes explicit that this analysis of Aboriginal right infringement applies directly to questions of treaty right infringement as well.[131]

This element of the test is a difficult aspect to undertake because the questions asked are almost entirely qualitative: unreasonableness and undue hardship. These are difficult standards to measure conduct against. However, the jurisprudence provides examples that can be used as benchmarks.

In *Sparrow* itself, the SCC found that a failure to give priority to Aboriginal fishers after valid conservation measures had been implemented was an infringement of the Musqueam Nation's Aboriginal right to fish.[132] In *Marshall No 1*, the Court came to a very similar conclusion in a treaty context, finding that "the purported regulatory prohibitions against fishing without a licence ... and of selling eels without a licence ... do *prima facie* infringe the appellant's treaty rights under the Treaties of 1760-61."[133] In *R v Adams*, the SCC determined that any "broad, unstructured administrative discretion" that "may carry significant consequences for the exercise of an [A]boriginal right" is a prima facie infringement unless it includes specific guidelines for the exercise of such discretion.[134] In *Badger*, the Court held that "there can be no limitation on the method, timing and extent of Indian hunting under a Treaty" but determined that safety regulations or requirements do not infringe treaty or Aboriginal rights.[135]

It would appear from the above that proving an infringement is not a high bar. If an infringement is proven, the court moves to a duty to consult analysis.

Duty to Consult and Accommodate

Fourth, the court must undertake the duty to consult and accommodate analysis. Although *Sparrow* speaks of consultation in the context of the justification analysis, this treatise separates these analyses based on *Mikisew Cree*. In that case, the SCC found that contemplated Crown action could "trigger" the duty to consult and accommodate within the context of the *Badger* test.[136] By referring to the trigger and by invoking *Haida Nation*'s duty to consult — as opposed to the less stringent question in *Sparrow*, which simply asks "whether the [A]boriginal group in question has been consulted"[137] as an aspect of justification — *Mikisew Cree* implies that, where specifically triggered by the test from *Haida Nation* or *Rio Tinto Alcan*, the duty to consult forms a separate part of the analysis. To reiterate, the duty to consult is triggered by (1) the Crown's knowledge, actual or constructive, of a potential Aboriginal claim or right; (2) contemplated Crown conduct; and (3) the potential that the contemplated conduct may adversely affect an Aboriginal claim or right.[138]

Where triggered, the duty to consult is assessed via the same principles as explicated above in this chapter. The threshold to trigger the duty is low, especially in the treaty context, where the first element — Crown knowledge of an Aboriginal claim or right — can be essentially presumed.[139]

Justification

Fifth and finally, if an infringement is found, the court must consider whether it is justified. As the SCC determined in *Badger*, the wording of section 35 — which protects both Aboriginal and treaty rights — supports "a common approach to infringements" of both types of rights.[140] Therefore, we return directly to *Sparrow*'s analysis.

According to *Sparrow*, the justification analysis proceeds in two stages. First, the court must ask whether the impugned legislation or decision has a valid legislative objective.[141] Second, the court must ask whether the impugned legislation or decision is consistent with the honour of the Crown, including its subsidiary doctrines the fiduciary duty, the duty to deal honourably, the duty to consult, and the duty of purposive and diligent fulfillment.[142]

In determining whether a legislative objective is valid, the SCC directs courts to scrutinize the objectives behind the legislation as well. For example, the curtailment of fishing or hunting in a particular territory might infringe a treaty-protected right to harvest, but it will be valid if the objective of the limitations is ultimately to preserve the treaty right to harvest "by conserving and managing a natural resource."[143] The court demands specificity in determining a legislative objective; it rejects "public interest" as justification, finding it to be "so vague as to provide no meaningful guidance and so broad as to be unworkable as a test for the justification of a limitation on constitutional rights."[144]

In determining whether the impugned legislation or decision is consistent with the honour of the Crown, the analysis typically centres around the fiduciary duty and often leads to a balancing of rights against each other. In *Sparrow*, the SCC acknowledged that, where resources are concerned, there may be many disparate claims of rights to them but determined that the constitutional guarantee of section 35 creates a special responsibility to allocate priority to Aboriginal rights or treaty rights holders.[145]

Other questions also need to be asked to determine whether the honour of the Crown is preserved. *Sparrow* suggested two: has the right been infringed as little as possible? and, in an expropriation, has proper compensation been made available?[146] In *R v Gladstone*, the SCC suggested that in determining whether an infringement is justified in a harvesting context, the importance of the resource to the Indigenous Nation and its way of life is a factor worthy of consideration.[147]

The idea that a treaty infringement can ever be justified has come in for criticism. This treatise earlier raised the idea that a justification analysis might never be appropriate within a treaty context based on the nature of treaty agreements: nation-to-nation bargains do not lend themselves to one nation bearing unilateral responsibility for interpretation and application. But the jurisprudence reveals a specific criticism of the procedure utilized to determine the justification of a treaty infringement. In dissent in *R v Van der Peet*, McLachlin J (as she then was) pointed out that the justification analysis is "judicially the equivalent" of the *Canadian Charter of Rights and Freedoms'* section 1 analysis,[148] which utilizes the *Oakes* test to determine if any infringement of an individual's *Charter* right is justifiable in a free and democratic society.[149] Applying this analysis to section 35 is inappropriate, however, because section 35 lies outside the *Charter*. In placing the section where they did in the *Constitution Act, 1982*, "the framers of s. 35(1) deliberately chose not to subordinate the exercise of [A]boriginal rights to the good of society as a whole."[150] Justice McLachlin suggested that only limitations "essential to its continued use and exploitation" of a resource based on a treaty or Aboriginal right should be considered justifiable.[151]

One final thing to bear in mind while conducting a justification analysis is that much of the jurisprudence on justification stems from the Aboriginal rights context. Although this jurisprudence is wholly applicable to the treaty context, *Badger* provided a hint that justification in the treaty context bears a somewhat higher onus when Cory J wrote, "[I]t is equally *if not more important* to justify *prima facie* infringements of treaty rights."[152]

CHAPTER FOUR

On the Breach of Treaties

Despite the fact that their dictionary definitions are similar, Canadian law treats infringement and breach of treaty as separate, but related, concepts. The easiest way to think about the relationship between the two is that all breaches are infringements, but not all infringements are breaches. The courts typically consider an infringement in the context of a law or an administrative decision that restricts or regulates a treaty right without necessarily removing it entirely. An infringement can be justified based on the analysis in Chapter 3. A breach is typically considered where Crown conduct violates or fails to fulfill an explicit term of a treaty — oral or written — or violates a doctrine related to treaty fulfillment, such as the honour of the Crown or the fiduciary duty. A breach cannot be justified.

Canadian jurisprudence offers few examples of courts finding a treaty breach *simpliciter*. Rather, courts often rest their decisions on breaches of related doctrines, such as the honour of the Crown or the fiduciary duty. It is not easily discernible why the Canadian judiciary is reticent to determine a breach of treaty. It may be based on an overall lack of facility with Crown-Indigenous treaty principles, or it may be that the related doctrines — being equitable rather than legal — open the door to equitable remedies, the flexibility of which judges see as an advantage when determining relief.

Recognized Breaches

Failure to Fulfill Treaty Entitlements

Breaches of this type deal with a failure to provide land or other items promised directly in treaty texts. Typically, these breaches will deal with reserve land entitlement based on a historical formula but may also deal with entitlement to annuities, the failure to provide farming implements, or the failure to provide medical care or supplies.

Jim Shot Both Sides v Canada is an example of a land entitlement claim.[1] The action concerned the amount of land that ought to have been reserved for the Blood Tribe in Blood Tribe Reserve No. 148, created pursuant to Treaty No. 7. Most numbered treaties created reserves based on a formula that accorded land based on a per person calculation. In Treaty No. 7, the formula was "one square mile for each family of five persons, or in that proportion for larger and smaller families."[2] Treaty No. 7 was signed in 1877, but the Blood Reserve was not surveyed until 1882. The problem occurred in 1883, when the reserve was surveyed a second time. The number of people living on the territory was smaller in 1883 than it had been in 1882, and the Crown moved the boundary of the reserve northward, reducing the reserve by 102.5 square miles.[3] The Blood Tribe alleged that this breached the treaty. The Crown argued that the first survey was merely preliminary and did not create the reserve, but the court rejected this, based partly on evidence that a number of officials in the Department of Indian Affairs considered the reserve boundaries finalized by the first survey. The Federal Court found a breach of treaty in addition to breaches of related duties.[4]

In *Restoule v Canada (Attorney General)*, the court was called upon to determine a more complicated issue: the potential increase of an annuity under treaty. A number of Anishinaabe First Nations in the upper Great Lakes region — signatories to the Robinson-Huron or Robinson-Superior treaties — alleged that the Crown had not fulfilled its promise to increase annuities paid to individual members of the Nations that had taken treaty. Signed in 1850, each treaty provided for

an individual annuity of approximately $1.65,[5] but the treaties them-
selves included an augmentation clause. This clause was the same in
each treaty and read, in part:

> The said William Benjamin Robinson, on behalf of Her Majesty,
> who desires to deal liberally and justly with all Her subjects, further
> promises and agrees that *in case the territory hereby ceded by the parties of*
> *the second part shall at any future period produce an amount which will enable*
> *the Government of this Province, without incurring loss, to increase the annuity*
> *hereby secured to them, then and in that case the same shall be augmented from*
> *time to time,* provided that the amount paid to each individual shall
> not exceed the sum of one pound Provincial currency in any one
> year, or such further sum as Her Majesty may be graciously pleased
> to order.[6]

The first and only time treaty annuities had been increased in the
manner described in the treaty was 1875, when the annuity increased
to $4 per person.[7] The annuity then remained at $4 per person for
nearly 150 years. At trial, the judge found this entitlement breached.
The Court of Appeal for Ontario concurred[8] and framed the trial
judge's findings on the issue in this way:

> [T]he trial judge held that the Crown has a mandatory and reviewable
> obligation to increase the Robinson Treaties' annuities. She found
> that the Crown must engage in a consultative process with the Treaty
> beneficiaries and pay an increased annuity amount, reflecting a "fair
> share," if there are sufficient Crown resource-based revenues to allow
> payment without incurring loss. The trial judge interpreted the £1
> (or $4) limit in the Treaties' augmentation clause to apply only to
> "distributive" payments to individuals, not as a limit or cap on the
> total collective annuity.[9]

In determining that the Crown had failed to fulfill a treaty entitlement, the trial court and court of appeal rested their reasoning on
both the text of the treaty and the duty to diligently implement treaty
promises.[10]

Breach of Textual Promise

Treaties contain a variety of promises, some that demand action and others that demand the restraint of action, either by the Crown or the settlers it governs. When the Crown does something it promised it would not or fails to do something it promised it would, it breaches the text of the treaty.

Saugeen First Nation v The Attorney General of Canada is an example of the latter. In that case, two Anishinaabe First Nations alleged, among other things, that the Crown had breached the most important clause in Treaty No. 45½, signed in 1836, known as the encroachment clause. During negotiations, the Crown asked the Saugeen to vacate their territory on Ontario's Bruce Peninsula and join other Anishinaabe groups on Manitoulin Island in order to open the peninsula to European settlement. The Saugeen refused. Instead, the Crown asked them to move further north on the peninsula, opening up more than a million acres to settlement and leaving the Saugeen with 450,000 acres of their traditional territory. The Saugeen agreed in return for a promise that the remaining land would "for ever" be protected for them "from the encroachments of the whites."[11] By 1854, however, the Crown returned, seeking the surrender of the remainder of the peninsula and citing the Crown's inability to control squatting on the reserved lands.[12] This led to the signing of Treaty No. 72, where the Saugeen surrendered the remainder of their lands, except for a few small reserves. Resting much of her reasoning on the Crown's failure to diligently fulfill the encroachment clause by not doing enough to curb squatting, Matheson J found that the treaty's encroachment clause had been breached.[13]

Despite their comprehensive nature and lengthy negotiations, modern treaties are also capable of textual breaches. *Nunavut Tunngavik Incorporated v Canada (Attorney General)* provides an example of the Crown's failure to diligently implement a textual promise. Having concluded the Nunavut Land Claims Agreement with the Crown in 1993, the Inuit of Nunavut alleged in 2006 that Article 12.7.6 of the agreement had been breached.[14] In that article, the Crown agreed to be responsible for "developing a general monitoring plan and for directing and co-ordinating general monitoring and data collection" in the interests of the health of the ecosystem,[15] although no date was specified for when the plan would be completed. No plan was developed by the time the suit was brought, although one was developed by 2010.[16] This was not diligent enough for the case management judge, who ruled in summary judgment that the Crown was obliged to develop the general monitoring plan by 2003 at the latest and was in breach of the treaty for having failed to do so.[17] Although aspects of the case were overturned on appeal, the Crown did not contest the finding of breach.[18]

Breach Caused by Cumulative Effects

In *Yahey v British Columbia*, the court was faced with a novel argument. Blueberry River First Nations, adherents to Treaty No. 8, argued that the cumulative effects of a number of industrial development projects, approved by the provincial Crown, had breached the First Nations' treaty rights to hunt and fish throughout their traditional territory. The Crown argued that the taking-up clause in Treaty No. 8 — which allowed the Crown to "take up land from time to time for settlement, mining, lumbering, trading and other purposes" — was a complete defence; the Crown, after all, had made clear to the ancestors of Blueberry River First Nations that a "period of transition" was dawning, which would have a "profound effect" on the way of life of the treaty's adherents.[19] The court rejected this position and found that the cumulative effects had left Blueberry River First Nations with no "meaningful" right to hunt and fish and therefore breached the treaty.[20]

In so doing, the court first had to contend with the language of the *Sparrow* test (see Chapter 3) to justify an infringement of treaty rights and its interpretation in *Mikisew Cree First Nation v Canada (Minister of Canadian Heritage)*. As the court in *Yahey* pointed out, *Mikisew Cree* left the door open to a cumulative effects claim when Binnie J determined that although not every taking up of land will constitute a treaty infringement, "if the time comes" that a First Nation can no longer meaningfully exercise a treaty right, the treaty is breached.[21] The problem is how to determine where that line is drawn: how can a court protect a right when it is diminished little by little, with each diminishment not constituting a breach in and of itself? As the court determined, the test for infringement must take the context of prior infringements into account; to neglect to do so risks creating "an artificial construct that does not fit with the reality of cumulative impacts resulting from industrial or other types of development today."[22]

Another issue that arises in *Yahey* is the content of the term "meaningful." As explained above, the court concluded that a treaty is breached by cumulative effects when there is no longer a way to exercise a treaty right "meaningfully." Meaningful, in the context of an Indigenous Nation, the court concluded, is "grounded in a way of life" and therefore must be viewed from the perspective of the Indigenous Nation.[23] Viewed from this perspective, the court concluded that the focus of the analysis must be "whether the treaty rights can be *meaningfully* exercised, not on whether the rights can be exercised *at all*."[24]

Remedies for Treaty Breach

What remedy is available for a breach of treaty is dependent on the type of breach and the context of the case.

Declaration

In *Manitoba Metis Federation Inc v Canada (Attorney General)*, the Supreme Court of Canada (SCC) ruled that a provision of the *Manitoba Act* was not implemented in accordance with the honour of the Crown and, because of the constitutional nature of the Act, issued the following declaration:

> That the federal Crown failed to implement the land grant provision set out in s. 31 of the *Manitoba Act, 1870* in accordance with the honour of the Crown.[25]

The Crown in *Manitoba Metis Federation* had argued that any relief for a failure to implement the obligations contained in the *Manitoba Act* was barred by the provincial statute of limitations or by laches, considering that it had been nearly 150 years since the *Manitoba Act* came into effect.[26] The court's willingness to grant a declaration in the face of such an argument rested on two principles. The first is that a declaration is a "narrow remedy" that "is not awarded against the defendant in the same sense as coercive relief."[27] The Court went so far as to say, "Were the Métis in this action seeking personal remedies, the reasoning set out here would not be available."[28] The second, and perhaps more important, reason is the fact that the "courts are the guardians of the Constitution" and therefore "cannot be barred by mere statutes from issuing a declaration on a fundamental constitutional matter."[29]

Although *Manitoba Metis Federation* was determined in regard to a constitutional promise, its principles are equally applicable to a treaty breach, for two reasons. First, the Court determined that the section of the *Manitoba Act* at issue is directly comparable to a treaty and even invoked the test from *R v Sioui*:[30]

> To understand the nature of s. 31 as a solemn obligation, it may be helpful to consider its treaty-like history and character. Section 31 sets out solemn promises — promises which are no less fundamental than treaty promises. Section 31, like a treaty, was adopted with "the intention to create obligations . . . and a certain measure of solemnity": *Sioui*, at p. 1044; *Sundown*. It was intended to create legal obligations of the highest order: no greater solemnity than inclusion in the Constitution of Canada can be conceived. Section 31 was conceived in the context of negotiations to create the new province of Manitoba. And all this was done to the end of reconciling the Métis Aboriginal interest with the Crown's claim to sovereignty.[31]

Second, as this treatise suggested in Chapter 1, the affirmation of treaty rights in section 35 of the *Constitution Act, 1982*[32] effectively constitutionalizes them, making a breach of treaty a constitutional issue about which the courts are free to make declarations.

Litigants should bear in mind that the type of declaration pleaded for is an important aspect of a case. In *Saugeen First Nation*, despite determining that both a textual promise in Treaty No. 45½ and the honour of the Crown were breached by the Crown's conduct, the trial judge noted that the plaintiffs sought "a declaration that the honour of the Crown was breached, not that the treaty was breached"; therefore, the declaration granted focused solely on the breach of the honour of the Crown.[33]

Stay of Proceedings

In limited circumstances — typically a regulatory prosecution, but potentially a criminal prosecution — a treaty breach may be remedied by staying proceedings against an accused.

In *R v Wolfe*, the Government of Saskatchewan attempted to address concerns about the illegal trafficking of wild meat on the Onion Lake Reserve in Treaty No. 6 territory through an undercover operation.[34] A conservation officer posed as a taxi driver and visited a Lloydminster, Saskatchewan, bar, where he made inquiries about purchasing wild meat; by doing so, he met one of the accused and proceeded to purchase a round of drinks in an effort to gain his trust and friendship. Over the course of a number of months, the officer visited with the accused and a number of others in their homes on the reserve. He typically brought alcohol onto the reserve with him, which he would share with the people he was investigating, and he often bought wild meat from them, in breach of conservation regulations. The investigation resulted in charges against four men, all citizens of Onion Lake Cree Nation.

As a defence, the accused sought to propound Treaty No. 6, which contained a clause banning alcohol on reserves.[35] The Court of Appeal cited and interpreted the clause in the following way:

> The provision establishing the alcohol ban provides:
>
> > Her Majesty further agrees with Her said Indians that within the boundary of Indian Reserves, until otherwise determined by Her Government of the Dominion of Canada, no intoxicating liquor shall be allowed to be introduced or sold, and all laws now in force, or hereafter to be enacted, to preserve her Indian subjects inhabiting the reserves or living elsewhere within Her Northwest Territories from the evil influence of the use of intoxicating liquors shall be strictly enforced.
>
> Thus, the Crown agreed that:
> 1. no alcohol would be allowed to be introduced or sold on reserves;
> 2. all present and future laws enacted for the purpose of protecting Indians from alcohol would be strictly enforced;
>
> *unless otherwise determined* by the Crown.[36]

The Crown argued that section 85.1 of the *Indian Act*[37] — enacted in 1985 and which allowed First Nations to make their own laws regarding the use, possession, or sale of alcohol — fulfilled any obligation from Treaty No. 6, such that the conservation officer's conduct merely violated the Onion Lake Cree Nation's bylaw against alcohol possession and supply, not the treaty itself.[38]

The court disagreed. It determined that, based on the commitment in Treaty No. 6 to strictly enforce "all present and future laws enacted for the purpose of protecting Indians from alcohol," and the fact that Onion Lake Cree Nation had enacted its own bylaw under section 85.1 of the *Indian Act*, the Crown had breached its treaty promise by failing to strictly enforce the bylaw.[39]

The treaty breach in and of itself did not lead to the stay of proceedings, however; rather, the conduct of the conservation officer in breaching the treaty had to rise to the level of an abuse of process in order for a stay to be warranted. The court reasoned:

> It is evident that not every treaty breach effected in the course of a criminal investigation warrants a stay. Whether a stay should be ordered depends on the facts of each case and can, as has already been stated, be ordered only in the "clearest of cases." Availability of the remedy depends on the relative significance of the treaty obligation sought to be upheld, the nature and degree of the breach, the nature of the offence, the seriousness of the infraction itself, and the relationship between the facts giving rise to the conviction and the penalty. What is at stake is society's interests in obtaining a conviction, considered in all the circumstances of the case, weighed against its obligation to uphold the treaty.[40]

Therefore, a test emerges from *Wolfe*:

> In criminal or regulatory prosecutions, a stay of proceedings is available as a remedy for a Crown breach of treaty rights, where appropriate. Appropriateness of the remedy is determined by weighing these factors:
> 1. The relative significance of the treaty obligation to the community at issue
> 2. The nature and degree of the breach

3. The nature of the offence
4. The seriousness of the infraction, and
5. The relationship between the facts giving rise to the conviction and the penalty

against the Crown's obligation to uphold the treaty.

Because it is highly dependent on a specific context, and because the test offers a relatively high threshold, a stay of proceedings is likely a rare remedy to a treaty breach.

Equitable Compensation

Equitable compensation is, as the name implies, compensation for a wrong based in equity. In the Indigenous context, it is typically a remedy for a breach of fiduciary duty — an equitable doctrine. It is not available solely for a breach of treaty; there must be a breach of an equitable doctrine as well. Most treaty breaches will also breach the fiduciary duty, but the possibility exists that a treaty breach will not do so; therefore, this is important to keep in mind.

Also important to keep in mind at the outset is that equitable compensation is a restitutionary remedy: it aims to restore to the beneficiary what was lost via the fiduciary's breach.[41] Where a beneficiary's loss can be restored *in specie*, equity would prefer that remedy as it restores exactly what was lost.[42] However, if the fiduciary's breach led to a loss that cannot be remedied *in specie*, equitable compensation will restore the value of what was lost, including reasonable increases to that value.

The first step in applying equitable compensation is determining that equitable compensation is the appropriate remedy. This may seem circular, but the remedy for any breach of fiduciary duty takes into account both the nature of the fiduciary's obligation and the nature of the breach. As Karakatsanis J wrote in *Southwind v Canada*, "There must be a close relationship between the fiduciary duty and the fiduciary remedy."[43] Only if the nature of the obligation and the nature of the breach point toward equitable compensation as the most appropriate remedy — rather than other equitable or legal remedies — will a court see fit to grant such relief.

In considering the nature of the obligation in a treaty context, courts have turned to contract, as happened in the trial-level decision in *Restoule*, which considered whether a treaty promise to augment annuities "if revenues received from the territory permitted the government to do so without incurring loss"[44] was a discretionary or a mandatory obligation. The trial judge wrote:

> I am not at all convinced that the presence of interpreters could or should have given Robinson confidence that the Chiefs understood the concepts of discretion, royal prerogative, or Her Majesty's graciousness, if such concepts had been embedded into the Treaties. And, therefore, *such concepts could not have informed the common intention of the parties.*[45]

The Ontario Court of Appeal largely agreed with her, essentially reading into her reasons the concept of "unfettered" discretion, and ruled that she "did not err in her analysis of the form and content of the Crown's discretion, or the First Nation's understanding of the scope of that discretion."[46]

However, as this treatise has insisted, treaties are not contracts. Therefore, the nature of the obligation must be different, and the jurisprudence suggests that it is a higher obligation than that created by contract.[47] This, the SCC explained in *Southwind*, is based on the fact that a fiduciary relationship will not typically exist between legal equals:

> In negligence and contract the parties were taken to be independent and equal actors, concerned primarily with their own self-interest. Consequently, the law sought a balance between enforcing obligations by awarding compensation, and preserving optimum freedom for those involved in the relationship. The essence of a fiduciary relationship, by contrast, was that one party pledged herself to act in the best interests of the other. The freedom of the fiduciary was diminished by the nature of the obligation she had undertaken. The fiduciary relationship had trust, not self-interest, at its core.[48]

Because the nature of the Crown's obligation is based in treaty and in the fiduciary duty, it can essentially be presumed. A "treaty promise is a Crown obligation of the highest order,"[49] which has been characterized as "sacred" or "solemn" on multiple occasions by the SCC;[50] therefore, the nature of the obligation "calls for the most honourable standard of fiduciary conduct."[51]

The nature of the breach analysis is a fact-focused investigation. When adjudicators analyze the nature of the breach, they typically describe the actions or inactions that caused the breach; the focus on the breach — rather than the loss — is indicative of a major difference between equitable compensation and common law damages. Because equity's concern is "not only to compensate the plaintiff, but to enforce the trust which is at its heart,"[52] the breach must violate that trust in order for a court to conclude that equitable compensation is an appropriate remedy. For example, in *Beardy's and Okemasis Band #96 and #97 v Her Majesty the Queen in Right of Canada*, Slade J described the breach within the context of the obligation, writing, "The Crown withheld money due to the Claimant under the most solemn of commitments, a treaty."[53] In another case, the same judge described the nature of a breach as "the failure to protect the Claimant's interest in access to the fishery."[54] In *Southwind*, Karakatsanis J described the nature of the breach as a failure "to negotiate compensation based upon the best price that could have been obtained."[55]

Having determined the nature of the obligation and described the nature of the breach, it is up to the adjudicator to decide if these factors point toward equitable compensation as the appropriate remedy.[56] If they do, the adjudicator next applies the principles of equitable compensation. These principles were recently restated in *Southwind*:

> In summary, equitable compensation deters wrongful conduct by fiduciaries in order to enforce the relationship at the heart of the fiduciary duty. It restores the opportunity that the plaintiff lost as a result of the fiduciary's breach. The trial judge must begin by closely analyzing the nature of the fiduciary relationship so as to ensure that the loss is assessed in relation to the obligations undertaken by the fiduciary. The loss must be caused in fact by the fiduciary's breach, but the causation analysis will not import foreseeability into breaches of the Crown's fiduciary duty towards Indigenous Peoples. Equitable presumptions — including most favourable use — apply to

the assessment of the loss. The most favourable use must be realistic. The trial judge must be satisfied that the assessment reflects the value the beneficiary could have actually received from the asset between breach and trial and the importance of the relationship between the Crown and Indigenous Peoples.[57]

From this, it is clear that to determine appropriate equitable compensation, an adjudicator must undertake three steps:

1. Causation analysis
2. Application of equitable presumptions
3. Assessment

These will be explored in turn.

CAUSATION

It is uncontroversial to say that for equitable compensation for a fiduciary breach to be an appropriate remedy, "there must be factual causation."[58] In other words, the breach must have caused a loss — including, potentially, lost opportunity.[59] Factual causation raises the spectre of the common law, but there are major differences in the causation analysis between equity and law, and equity's causation analysis is the only appropriate one when an adjudicator has determined that equitable compensation is the appropriate remedy.

Chief among these differences is the fact that "common law limiting factors will not readily apply because of the nature of the fiduciary relationship and obligations."[60] The reason for this, again, is related to the nature of a fiduciary's obligation; as mentioned, whereas a contract is entered into by legal equals, vulnerability and trust are at the heart of the fiduciary relationship.[61] Therefore, although a fiduciary's breach must factually cause a beneficiary's loss, common law rules having to do with causation — such as foreseeability and remoteness — do not apply to equitable compensation.[62]

Connected to the concept of foreseeability, and which will also be important to the assessment analysis, is the ability to use hindsight to measure loss. Whereas the common law measures damages foreseeable at the date of breach, equitable compensation measures a loss "at the date of trial on the basis of facts known at trial,"[63] including any unforeseeable increase in the value of the property between the breach and the trial. This also allows for a more robust causation analysis because the true losses connected to the breach via evidence — not simply those foreseeable at the time of the breach — are to be compensated for. This is also connected to the restitutionary nature of equitable compensation: the goal is to "restore the plaintiff to the position the plaintiff would have been in had the Crown not breached its duty," which includes gains that would have accumulated had the breach never occurred.[64]

Unlike foreseeability and remoteness, however, contributory negligence, mitigation, and apportionment may be relevant considerations in equitable compensation. This is an unsettled area of the law, however, and if an adjudicator determines that they indeed apply, care must be taken to consider these doctrines through the lenses of fairness and justice and the flexibility of equity. In *Canson Enterprises*, the decision and the concurrence were at odds on this topic. In the decision, La Forest J adopted the reasoning of a New Zealand case that rested the applicability of these doctrines on the historical fusion of law and equity.[65] He wrote that he would indeed apply doctrines of contributory negligence, mitigation, and apportionment because

> the maxims of equity can be flexibly adapted to serve the ends of justice as perceived in our days. They are not rules that must be rigorously applied but malleable principles intended to serve the ends of fairness and justice.... [L]aw and equity have long overlapped in pursuit of their common goal of affording adequate remedies against those placed in a position of trust or confidence when they breach a duty that reasonably flows from that position.
>
> ...
>
> Only when there are different policy objectives should equity engage in its well-known flexibility to achieve a different and fairer result.[66]

Justice McLachlin disagreed. Although she would "readily concede that we may take wisdom where we find it," she did not feel that analogy to common law was appropriate because "it overlooks the unique foundation and goals of equity."[67] She went so far as to say that, in equity, "The plaintiff will not be required to mitigate ..., but losses resulting from clearly unreasonable behaviour on the part of the plaintiff will be adjudged to flow from that behaviour, and not from the breach."[68] Justice La Forest's mixing of the doctrines risked an illogical result because "it appears that he would treat benefit to the fiduciary on the basis of equitable principles, and losses to the plaintiff on the basis of common law."[69] Instead, she wrote, "[I]t is preferable to deal with both remedies under the same system — equity."[70] The unique foundation of equity, according to McLachlin J (as she then was), is that it "has trust, not self-interest, at its core"; therefore, when a breach does occur, "the balance favours the person wronged."[71] Favouring the person wronged in order to enforce the trust at the heart of the fiduciary relationship, it would seem, means typically choosing not to apply common law doctrines that would reduce compensation — including contributory negligence, mitigation, and apportionment.[72] Justice McLachlin's less permissive approach has been followed subsequently in some courts, and the differences between the decision and the concurrence in *Canson Enterprises* were well canvassed by Gray J in *Lemberg v Perris*.[73] Ultimately, the judge favoured McLachlin J's approach, writing:

> While it may not be appropriate to directly apply the concept of contributory negligence to the calculation of losses flowing from a breach of fiduciary duty ... as adopted by La Forest J. in *Canson*, it may be appropriate to apply the concept by analogy where it is equitable to do so. That is how I read the judgment of McLachlin J. in *Canson*. At the end of the day, *the question is whether it is equitable, in the particular circumstances of the case, to reduce the recovery of the plaintiff because he or she failed to take some reasonable step that might have reduced or eliminated the loss.*[74]

Despite the plaintiffs' opportunity to mitigate their losses in *Lemberg*, Gray J ruled against applying mitigation, writing, "I do not think the plaintiffs' compensation should be reduced because, in 20/20 hindsight, the plaintiffs might have ignored Mr. Perris's advice and done something different."[75]

In the trial decision in *Southwind v Canada*, the Federal Court went so far as to say, "Despite writing for the minority in both cases, Justice McLachlin's view of the principles of equitable compensation ... has since become accepted in Canada and elsewhere."[76] This *obiter dicta* is, however, cited to a case from the United Kingdom.

To reiterate, there must be some evidence that a fiduciary's breach has factually caused a loss to the beneficiary. Where evidence shows factual causation, hindsight allows a court to ascertain all of the losses caused by the breach to the date of trial, and this analysis is not limited by foreseeability or remoteness. The analysis may be limited by doctrines such as contributory negligence, mitigation, and apportionment, but only where applying these doctrines is equitable.

EQUITABLE PRESUMPTIONS

Again connected to the idea that equitable compensation enforces the trust at the heart of the fiduciary duty,[77] at the second stage of determining appropriate compensation, the court applies equitable presumptions to the evidence. Chief among these is the presumption that a beneficiary would have made "the most favourable use" of the property lost via the breach.[78]

The most favourable use is determined via evidence and hindsight. Evidence — often presented by expert witnesses — can be lead as to what the best use of an asset would have been based on economic conditions as they really were, and, again, the foreseeability of changed economic conditions or the value of an asset is not an appropriate consideration. For example, in *Southwind*, the SCC determined that the most favourable use of the property was as a dam for hydroelectricity generation, despite the fact that at the time the land was taken, the First Nation could not have reasonably known the land's most economically favourable use.[79] This lack of knowledge was connected directly to the breach, with the Court commenting that "if ... Canada had fulfilled its fiduciary obligations, the [Lac Seul First Nation] would have gone into the negotiations fully informed of the significant value of its land to the Project."[80] Because the most favourable use was for hydroelectricity generation, the Court determined that "equitable compensation must reflect Canada's obligation to ensure the [Lac Seul First Nation] was compensated for the value of the land to the Project," not simply compensated for the value that could have been negotiated at the time.[81] The concept of most favourable use does have limits, however, as the SCC said in *Southwind*:

> The most favourable use must be realistic. The trial judge must be satisfied that the assessment reflects the value the beneficiary could have actually received from the asset between breach and trial and the importance of the relationship between the Crown and Indigenous Peoples.[82]

For example, in *Beardy's*, the Specific Claims Tribunal rejected the evidence of a claimant's expert on the basis that it was unrealistic. The expert determined that annuity money that had been illegally withheld from the members of the First Nation from 1885 to 1888 following the North-West Rebellion could have generated up to $2.5 billion had it been invested perfectly — a level of investment efficiency possible through the benefit of hindsight.[83] In addition to being significantly over the tribunal's statutory compensation limit, the expert's opinion was rejected because, as the tribunal determined, "To base an award on theoretically possible but extremely unlikely uses of the lost money, had it been received, is unrealistic."[84]

Two further presumptions apply to equitable compensation: the presumption of legality and the *Brickenden* rule.

The presumption of legality in equity is simply stated: the court is to presume that a fiduciary would have honoured its legal obligations.[85] As the court uses hindsight to determine what likely would have happened but for the breach, this presumption prevents fiduciaries from arguing that they would not have complied with the law and thus compensation should be reduced.[86] For example, in *Whitefish Lake Band of Indians v Canada (Attorney General)*, the Ontario Court of Appeal determined that, under the *Indian Act* in force at the time of a timber surrender, 90 percent of the revenue received should have been invested for the benefit of the First Nation, whereas 10 percent was to be received by members directly. Having failed to invest 90 percent of the $31,600 received, the court called this number the "starting point for fixing Whitefish's compensation."[87] Based on the presumption that the fiduciary would have followed the law, it was this amount — or, rather, 90 percent of the amount — that the court ruled needed to be brought forward to the present day by applying historical interest rates, compounded at the same rate as First Nations' capital accounts.[88]

The *Brickenden* rule stems, unsurprisingly, from *London Loan & Savings Company of Canada v Brickenden*, a decision of the Judicial Committee of the Privy Council.[89] The rule only applies in cases where a fiduciary has breached a duty to disclose material facts and prevents the fiduciary from arguing "that the outcome would be the same regardless of whether the facts were disclosed."[90]

ASSESSMENT

It is never more important than at the assessment stage to bear in mind equity's ultimate objective in providing compensation for breach of fiduciary duty — "putting the beneficiary in the position it would have been in but for the fiduciary's breach of duty."[91] As previously mentioned, in order to more accurately restore the beneficiary — and to avoid foreseeability issues — equitable compensation is assessed as of the date of trial "on the basis of facts known at trial," not the date of breach.[92] Unlike common law damages, equitable compensation is "a discretionary remedy that is assessed and not precisely calculated."[93] And although, as McLachlin J wrote in *Canson Enterprises*, "the balance favours the person wronged,"[94] in *Southwind*, the SCC determined that "assessment needs to be realistic."[95] Assessment can be broken down into three steps:

1. Determine a realistic starting point,
2. Apply realistic contingencies, and
3. Ensure that the deterrent function of equity is fulfilled.

A trial judge must find a realistic starting point from which to begin the assessment. The first step in determining the starting point is defining the fiduciary obligations applicable to the relationship.[96] Following this, the "trial judge assesses reasonable, or realistic, outcomes in light of those obligations," presuming, of course, that the fiduciary complied with their obligations, as well as presuming the most favourable use of what was lost in the breach with the benefit of hindsight.[97]

This may involve expert valuation evidence regarding the historical and/ or current value of lost property, may involve hypotheticals or proxy models of profit based on similar circumstances where the fiduciary duty was complied with,[98] or, in cases such as *Beardy's*, where annuity money was withheld, may simply be a calculation. Where a loss is historical, it will typically need to be brought forward to present-day value using compound interest, to account for the time value of money[99] and for the often ongoing nature of a fiduciary's breach,[100] although the awarding of compound interest is ultimately discretionary.[101] Where parties present competing expert evidence, the judge has the discretion to agree with one expert over another or agree with parts of one expert's evidence and parts of another's.

Having determined a realistic starting point, a court will next apply realistic contingencies to the proposed compensation. This process was described in *Southwind* as involving "the trial judge [taking] into account 'events that could have occurred had the fiduciary duty not been breached and that might have increased (or decreased) the value of what the beneficiary lost as a result of the breach.'"[102] Care should be taken not to double count a contingency for or against a plaintiff, however; for example, where compensation is based on the current ascertainable value of a historical loss of property, utilizing the current value "bakes in" any fluctuations in value over the time period in question. Alternatively, where a historical value is brought forward using compound interest, this number may need to be reduced — or increased — based on evidence of significant historical market fluctuations.

Before ruling upon the final compensation amount, a trial judge "must determine whether the new total compensation award is sufficient to fulfill the deterrent function of equity."[103] Punitive damages, although possible under the principles of equitable compensation, require conduct by the fiduciary that is "purposefully repugnant to the beneficiary's best interests" and "will be particularly applicable where the impugned activity is motivated by the fiduciary's self-interest."[104] Rather than make compensation awards that are punitive in nature, courts considering treaty breaches tend to lean on the deterrent function of equitable compensation to similar effect in Indigenous contexts. Deterrence has a "special importance" in Indigenous contexts "because deterring the Crown from breaching its fiduciary duty encourages it to act honourably and orients it towards the ongoing project of reconciliation."[105]

If the judge arrives at an equitable compensation amount that is realistic in context, takes into account realistic contingencies, and satisfies the need to deter future fiduciary breaches, the compensation award is appropriate. The ultimate goal is to provide a "global assessment" — not a precise mathematical calculation — that takes into account equity's goals and unique features while delivering a just result.[106]

Equitable Defences

Before leaving the topic of equitable compensation, a word on equitable defences is necessary: where equitable relief is claimed, equitable defences are applicable.

One area of particular interest is the equitable defence of laches. The elements of laches are relatively straightforward. There are two separate branches of the doctrine — waiver and prejudice — but these can be distilled into a single test as so:

Laches acts as a defence to an equitable claim where there is:

1. Unreasonable delay on the part of the plaintiff *and*
2a. The delay is equivalent to waiver of the conduct at issue *or*
2b. Prejudice to the defendant has arisen because they relied on the plaintiff's delay as proof of the acceptability of the status quo[107]

To put this test another way, two elements are necessary: for laches to apply, there must be delay that is unreasonable, coupled with either waiver or prejudice. Unlike a limitations period, no particular amount of delay is sufficient to trigger laches. As the SCC determined in *M(K) v M(H)*, "mere delay is insufficient to trigger laches"; there must be more.[108] This treatise will analyze the two necessary elements in turn.

UNREASONABLE DELAY

At least one commentator has suggested that twenty years might be considered a "convenient guide" for when delay becomes unreasonable under the doctrine of laches.[109] Caution is warranted, however, as the SCC noted in *M(K) v M(H)* that "laches must be resolved as a matter of justice as between the parties, as is the case with any equitable doctrine."[110] There are a vast number of exceptions to this rule of thumb. For example, in *KK v GKW*, a woman alleged a breach of fiduciary duty against her mother for allowing her father to repeatedly sexually molest her forty years previously, and the Ontario Court of Appeal refused to apply laches.[111] In *Manitoba Metis Federation*, faced with an equitable claim following more than a century of delay, the SCC similarly refused to apply laches to bar relief.[112]

What appears to really matter when a court must determine whether delay is "unreasonable" is the context of the delay.[113] In Indigenous contexts, delay in asserting legal rights is often explainable, and in the context of reconciliation, courts are less eager to apply laches to any amount of delay, especially if the Crown bears some responsibility. In *Chippewas of Sarnia Band v Canada (Attorney General)*, the Ontario Court of Appeal wrote:

> Aboriginal claims often arise from historical grievances. These claims reflect the disadvantages long suffered by [A]boriginal communities and the failure of our society and our legal system to provide adequate responses. There is a significant risk that denial of claims on grounds of delay will only add insult to injury. It is plainly not the law that [A]boriginal claims will be defeated on grounds of delay alone. The reason and any explanation for the delay must be carefully considered with due regard to the historically vulnerable position of [A]boriginal peoples.[114]

This could be considered a manifestation of the "clean hands" doctrine. Typically applied to bar plaintiffs from relief, the doctrine demands that a plaintiff seeking equitable relief come before the court with "clean hands" in the matter, having done nothing that might allow a person to conclude that the party seeking relief bears some of the blame in the situation. As per the Federal Court of Appeal in

Ling Chi Medicine Co (HK) v Persaud, the doctrine of clean hands also applies to a defendant seeking to rely on an equitable defence: "He who invokes an equitable defence must have done equity in respect of the same matter," the court wrote.[115]

The Canadian government appears to be cognizant of the issue. The Specific Claims Tribunal — a specialized federal tribunal that determines historical treaty breach and related claims from First Nations — does not allow laches as a defence, per its enabling Act:

Limitation

19 In deciding the issue of the validity of a specific claim, the Tribunal shall not consider any rule or doctrine that would have the effect of limiting claims or prescribing rights against the Crown because of the passage of time or delay.[116]

In *Canada v Stoney Band*, the plaintiff First Nation argued that using procedural defences such as laches to defeat a claim without considering its merits was, in and of itself, a breach of the honour of the Crown.[117] Deciding the case in 2005, and relying on *Wewaykum Indian Band v Canada*, which was decided in 2002, the Federal Court of Appeal did not accept the argument.[118] In more recent years, however, it appears to be gaining ground.

In Indigenous contexts, it may serve as an appropriate guide to interpret the phrase "unreasonable delay" in the test from *M(K) v M(H)* as "unexplainable delay," such that, where delay is reasonably explained, then, by definition, it is not unreasonable. Where delay is not unreasonable, the test is not fulfilled, and the adjudicator need not move onto the second stage. If delay is determined to be unreasonable, however, a decision maker moves onto the second stage of the test: waiver or prejudice.

WAIVER OR PREJUDICE

As mentioned previously, mere delay — even unreasonable delay — is not sufficient to trigger laches; both the first and second stages of the test must be fulfilled. It is very important to keep in mind at the test's second stage that the second stage is an either/or proposition: to fulfill the test from *M(K) v M(H)*, there must be (1) unreasonable delay coupled with either (2a) waiver or (2b) prejudice.

Waiver, also known as acquiescence, has "a significant knowledge requirement."[119] It is "not enough that a plaintiff knows of the facts that support a claim in equity"; they must "also know that the facts give rise to the claim," which requires some knowledge of a plaintiff's legal rights.[120] Or, as the SCC put it in *M(K) v M(H)*, "[T]he question is whether it is reasonable for a plaintiff to be ignorant of her legal rights given her knowledge of the underlying facts relevant to a possible legal claim."[121] Based on the almost complete control the Crown had on Indigenous life for long stretches of Canadian history — control that was exercised through the *Indian Act*, the Indian Agent, residential schools, access to higher education, the pass system, and the long-term ban on hiring lawyers and exacerbated by ongoing trauma as well as prior treaty breaches that led to depressed economic conditions — courts have been more willing to refuse to apply laches in recent years, noting that this level of control often resulted in a lack of "knowledge, capacity and freedom" to legally acquiesce to the status quo.[122] In other words, without knowledge that a legal claim is possible or the capacity to pursue it, laches is inapplicable.[123]

The prejudice branch is concerned with the position of the defendant or third parties, not with that of the plaintiff. It "requires unreasonable delay resulting in circumstances that make the prosecution of the action unreasonable."[124] What would make the prosecution of an action unreasonable? In *Chippewas of Sarnia Band*, the Ontario Court of Appeal determined that a large tract of reserve land had been transferred by Crown patent from a First Nation to an individual without a formal surrender,[125] which would typically be a violation of the *Indian Act* and/or the fiduciary duty. But the patented land had been sold to other settlers, who were not culpable for the Crown's breach. The court applied laches, ruling that "courts have a discretion to refuse a remedy with respect to the inadvertent error of a dysfunctional bureaucracy that has been relied on for 150 years by innocent third parties."[126] In *Wewaykum*, the SCC invoked improvements made over many years to lands that may have been improperly allocated to apply laches via the prejudice branch.[127] In *Manitoba Metis Federation*, the SCC refused to apply laches on either the waiver or prejudice branches, quoting *M(K) v M(H)* for the proposition that prejudice arises when a defendant alters "his position in reasonable reliance on the plaintiff's acceptance of the status quo" and ruling that the Crown had not altered its position.[128]

As this chapter has recounted, there is little law on treaty breach *simpliciter*. Courts tend to seek breaches of related doctrines such as the honour of the Crown or the fiduciary duty in order to find breaches in equity that open the door to equitable remedies. Where a true treaty breach is found, unlike in contract, the treaty is not subject to rescission. The breach may lead to a remedy, including a remedy in equity if an equitable breach is found, but the treaty will persist.

Notes

CHAPTER ONE | **On the Nature of Treaties**

1   See *R v Marshall*, [1999] 3 SCR 456 at para 78, 177 DLR (4th) 513 [*Marshall No 1*]; *Beckman v Little Salmon/Carmacks First Nation*, 2010 SCC 53 at para 10 [*Beckman*]; *R v Badger*, [1996] 1 SCR 771 at paras 76–78, 133 DLR (4th) 324 [*Badger*]; *R v Sundown*, [1999] 1 SCR 393 at para 24, 170 DLR (4th) 385 [*Sundown*].

2   *Badger*, above note 1 at para 76.

3   See, e.g., *Marshall No 1*, above note 1 at para 43.

4   *Badger*, above note 1 at para 76.

5   *Mikisew Cree First Nation v Canada (Governor General in Council)*, 2018 SCC 40 at para 5 [*Mikisew Cree*].

6   *Marshall No 1*, above note 1 at para 25.

7   *R v Sioui*, [1990] 1 SCR 1025, 70 DLR (4th) 427 [*Sioui*].

8   In *General Motors Corporation v Peco, Inc*, [2006] OJ No 636, 15 BLR (4th) 282 (SC), Cumming J defined contracts as "bundles of reciprocal reasonable expectations, created by the exchange of promises," at para 24. See also *Suen v Suen*, 2013 BCCA 313, where the British Columbia Court of Appeal defined a contract as "promissory in nature, that is, it is an undertaking by the promisor to do something for the promisee in exchange for something," at para 40.

9   Canada, Department of Indian Affairs, *Indian Treaties and Surrenders: From 1680 to 1890*, vol 1 (Ottawa: B Chamberlain, 1891) at 113.

10   Hon Alexander Morris, *The Treaties of Canada with the Indians of Manitoba and the North-West Territories* (Toronto: Willing & Williamson, 1880) at 96.

11   *Sioui*, above note 7 at para 56.

12   *Ibid* at paras 125–29.

13 *Ibid* at para 103.

14 *Simon v The Queen*, [1985] 2 SCR 387 at para 30, 24 DLR (4th) 390 [*Simon*].

15 Miguel Alfonso Martinez, *Study on Treaties, Agreements and Other Constructive Arrangements Between States and Indigenous Populations*, UNESCOR, 51st Sess, UN Doc E/CN.4/Sub.2/1999/20 at 30.

16 *Beckman*, above note 1 at para 10.

17 *Honouring the Truth, Reconciling for the Future: Summary of the Final Report of the Truth and Reconciliation Commission of Canada* (Ottawa, 2015) at 195.

18 *Indian Act*, RSC 1985, c I-5.

19 *Constitution Act, 1982*, being Schedule B to the *Canada Act 1982* (UK), 1982, c 11.

20 *Indian Act*, above note 18 at s 88.

21 *Constitution Act, 1867* (UK), 30 & 31 Vict, c 3, s 91(24), reprinted in RSC 1985, Appendix II, No 5.

22 *R v White* (1964), 50 DLR (2d) 613 at 616, 52 WWR (ns) 193 (BCCA) [*White*].

23 *Kruger et al v The Queen*, [1978] 1 SCR 104 at 110, 75 DLR (3d) 434.

24 *Game Act*, RSBC 1960, c 160.

25 *White*, above note 22 at 619.

26 *Sioui*, above note 7.

27 *R v Morris*, 2006 SCC 59 at para 2.

28 *Ibid* at para 35.

29 *Sundown*, above note 1.

30 *Simon*, above note 14 at para 31.

31 *Sundown*, above note 1 at para 33.

32 *Simon*, above note 14 at para 29.

33 *Rex v Syliboy*, [1929] 1 DLR 307 at para 21 (p 313), 4 CNLC 430 (NSSC) [*Syliboy*].

34 *Simon*, above note 14 at para 54.

35 *Badger*, above note 1 at para 79. See also *Sparrow*, below note 42.

36 *Constitution Act, 1982*, above note 19.

37 *Ibid*, at s 35(3), which reads: "For greater certainty, in subsection (1) 'treaty rights' includes rights that now exist by way of land claims agreements or may be so acquired."

38 *Quebec (Attorney General) v Moses*, 2010 SCC 17 at para 82 [*Moses*].

39 *Badger*, above note 1 at para 79. See also *R v Van der Peet*, [1996] 2 SCR 507 at para 28, 137 DLR (4th) 289 [*Van der Peet*].

40 *Canadian Charter of Rights and Freedoms*, Part I of the *Constitution Act, 1982*, being Schedule B to the *Canada Act 1982* (UK), 1982, c 11 [*Charter*].

41 *Van der Peet*, above note 39 at para 308, McLachlin J, dissenting.

42 *Ibid* at para 28; *R v Sparrow*, [1990] 1 SCR 1075, 70 DLR (4th) 385.

43 *Badger*, above note 1 at para 75.

44 *Yahey v British Columbia*, 2021 BCSC 1287 at para 451.

45 *Moses*, above note 38 at para 7.

46 See, e.g., John J. Borrows & Leonard I. Rotman, *Aboriginal Legal Issues: Cases, Materials & Commentary*, 5th ed (Toronto: LexisNexis, 2018) at 282–86, where the authors suggest the following types of treaty: (1) Indigenous treaties with the natural world; (2) Indigenous-to-Indigenous treaties; (3) commercial and personal treaties; (4) peace and friendship treaties; (5) territorial treaties; and (6) modern treaties.

47 *Marshall No 1*, above note 1 at para 5.

48 *Restoule v Canada (Attorney General)*, 2018 ONSC 7701 at para 65 [*Restoule*] [footnote omitted].

49 *Ibid* at para 95.

50 *Ibid.*

51 In *Lac La Ronge Indian Band v Canada*, 2001 SKCA 109, the Indigenous party sought a declaration that Canada had not fulfilled Treaty No. 6 because it had not transferred all the land set aside under the agreement to the First Nation. The major issue was whether it was the intentions of the parties, in a situation where it was alleged that the allotment had not been fully transferred, to determine the entitlement via the population of the First Nation at the time of signing or at present. The Court of Appeal determined that the terms of the agreement made took precedence: the entitlement under Treaty No. 6 was based on the First Nation's population at the time of the Nation's adherence to the agreement, in 1891. Having found that the Crown allotted sufficient land to fulfill the treaty based on the Nation's population in 1891, the court dismissed the First Nation's appeal.

52 In *Mikisew Cree First Nation v Canada (Minister of Canadian Heritage)*, 2005 SCC 69, despite the fact that the treaty at issue — Treaty No. 8 — included a clause that allowed the Crown to "take up" land from time to time seemingly without restriction, the SCC determined that it would not fulfill the purpose or meaning of the treaty to allow for unilateral action that affected the rights guaranteed to the First Nation by the agreement. The Crown, therefore, had a duty to consult the Cree about any action that would affect their rights as enumerated in the treaty.

53 *Badger*, above note 1 at paras 39–40.

54 *Ibid* at paras 53–54.

55 *Mikisew Cree*, above note 5 at para 5. The idea of an exchange of territory for guaranteed rights is reinforced in *Haida Nation v British Columbia (Minister of Forests)*, 2004 SCC 73 at para 20 [*Haida Nation*], where the SCC determines that a duty to consult an Indigenous claimant group exists even prior to treaty formation and that, when negotiations for such treaties are entered into, "the Crown [must] act honourably in defining the rights it *guarantees* and in reconciling them with other rights and interests" [emphasis added].

56 *Moses*, above note 38 at para 7.

57 *Ibid* at para 98.

58 *Ibid* at para 7.

59 See, e.g., the *James Bay and Northern Quebec Native Claims Settlement Act*, SC 1976-77, c 32, s 3(2)-(3).

60 *Sioui*, above note 7 at 1037.

61 *Ibid*.

62 *Sga'nism Sim'augit (Chief Mountain) v Canada (Attorney General)*, 2013 BCCA 49 at para 46.

63 *R v Vincent*, 12 OR (3d) 427 at para 34 (p 15-16), [1993] 2 CNLR 165 (CA) [Vincent]; *Mitchell v Minister of National Revenue*, [1997] 153 DLR (4th) 1 at para 263, [1997] 4 CNLR 103 (SCC).

64 *Ibid*.

65 *Francis v The Queen*, [1956] SCR 618 at para 35 (p 14), 3 DLR (2d) 641.

66 *White*, above note 22 at 617.

67 *Sioui*, above note 7 at 1037.

68 *Ibid* at 1038. See also *Simon*, above note 14 at para 21; *White*, above note 22 at para 120.

69 *Ibid* at paras 1040 & 1041.

70 *Syliboy*, above note 33.

71 *Ibid* at 313.

72 *Simon*, above note 14 at para 21.

73 *Ibid* at para 24 [emphasis added]. See also *Marshall No 1*, above note 1 at paras 27-29.

74 *Sioui*, above note 7 at 1057, quoting Captain John Knox, *An Historical Journal for the Campaigns in North America for the Years 1757, 1758, 1759, and 1760*, vol II (London: 1769) [emphasis added].

75 *Beckman*, above note 1 at para 10.

76 *Sioui*, above note 7 at para 40 (p 1042-42).

77 N.A.M. MacKenzie, "Indians and Treaties in Law" (1929) 7 *Canadian Bar Review* 561 at 565, quoted in *Syliboy*, above note 33 at para 20.

78 *Sioui*, above note 7 at 1038.

79 *Province of Ontario v The Dominion of Canada and Province of Quebec* (1895), 25 SCR 434 at 512, 1895 CanLII 112, Gwynne J, dissenting.

80 *Marshall No 1*, above note 1 at para 49. See also *Badger*, above note 1 at para 41.

81 *Haida Nation*, above note 55 at para 19, quoting *Badger*, above note 1.

82 *Westbank v BC (Minister of Forests) and Wenger*, [2000] 191 DLR (4th) 180 at para 65, [2001] 1 CNLR 361 (BCSC) [*Westbank*].

83 *Delgamuukw v British Columbia*, [1986] BCJ No 1413 at para 18 (BCCA); *Chemainus First Nation v British Columbia (Assets and Lands Corp)*, [1999] 3 CNLR 8 at para 26, [1999] BCJ No 682 (SC) [*Chemainus First Nation*]; *Westbank*, above note 82 at para 70.

84 *Chemainus First Nation*, above note 83 at para 26.

85 *Ibid.*

86 *Westbank*, above note 82 at para 74.

87 *Mohawks of the Bay of Quinte v Canada (Indian Affairs and Northern Development)*, 2013 FC 669 at paras 53 and 59.

88 *Badger*, above note 1 at para 41; see also *Westbank*, above note 82 at para 74; *Chemainus First Nation*, above note 83 at para 26.

89 *Marshall No 1* above note 1 at para 14.

90 *Sioui*, above note 7 at 1044.

91 *Moses*, above note 38 at para 97, quoting *Sioui*, above note 7 at 1044.

92 *Regina v Taylor and Williams* (1981), 34 OR (2d) 360, [1981] 3 CNLR 114 (CA) [*Taylor and Williams*].

93 *Sioui*, above note 7 at 1045.

94 *Ibid*, based on *Taylor and Williams*, above note 92 at paras 10–13 (p 8–10).

95 *Ibid* at 1031.

96 *Ibid* at para 76 (p 1056).

97 *Ibid* at 1057.

98 *Vincent*, above note 63.

99 *Ibid* at para 12.

100 *Ibid* at paras 34–37.

101 *Ibid* at paras 56–57.

102 *Ibid* at para 60.

103 *Sioui*, above note 7, at paras 83–87.

104 *Moses*, above note 38, at paras 106 and 20.

105 *Ibid* at para 98, Lebel J, dissenting, although not on this point.

106 *Ibid* at para 7.

107 *Simon*, above note 14 at para 6.

108 *Ibid* at para 24 [emphasis added].

109 *White*, above note 22.

110 *Ibid* at 649.

111 *Sioui*, above note 7 at 1045.

112 *Chippewas of Sarnia Band v Canada (Attorney General)* (2000), 51 OR (3d) 641 at para 60, 195 DLR (4th) 135 (CA).

113 *Ibid* at para 55; see also *R v Polchies*, [1982] 4 CNLR 167 at paras 9–12, [1982] NBJ No 132; *R c Côté*, [1993] RJQ 1350 at para 69, [1994] 3 CNLR 98, reversed in part, although not on the existence of the treaty, [1996] 3 SCR 139, 138 DLR (4th) 385.

114 *Sioui*, above note 7 at para 80 (p 1057); *Moses*, above note 38 at para 7.

115 *Jim Shot Both Sides v Canada*, 2019 FC 789 at para 70; *Restoule*, above note 48 at para 214; *Ermineskin v Canada*, 2005 FC 1623 at paras 91–93.

116 *Sundown*, above note 1 at para 11.

117 *Ibid* at para 29.

118 *Ibid* at para 30.

119 *Ibid* at para 36.

120 *R v Marshall*, [1999] 3 SCR 533 at para 17, [1999] 4 CNLR 301 [*Marshall No 2*].

121 *Gill v Canada*, 2005 FC 192 at para 13.

122 *Behn v Moulton Contracting Ltd*, 2013 SCC 26 at para 42 [*Behn*]. For an in-depth consideration of the *Behn* case, see Francesca Allodi-Ross, "Who Calls the Shots? Balancing Individual and Collective Interests in the Assertion of Aboriginal and Treaty Harvesting Rights" in John Borrows & Michael Coyle, eds, *The Right Relationship: Reimagining the Implementation of Historical Treaties* (Toronto: University of Toronto Press, 2017) at 149.

123 *Behn*, above note 122 at para 34.

124 *Ibid* at para 34.

125 *Ibid* at para 35.

126 *Papaschase Indian Band (Descendants of) v Canada (Attorney General)*, 2004 ABQB 655 at para 175.

127 *Soldier v Canada (Attorney General)*, 2009 MBCA 12 at para 55 [*Soldier*].

128 *Ibid* at para 52.

129 *Restoule*, above note 48 at paras 401–2.

130 *Ibid* at paras 463–65.

131 *Simon*, above note 14 at para 31.

132 *Montana Band v Canada*, 2006 FC 261 [*Montana Band*].

133 *Ibid* at para 2.

134 *Ibid* at para 25.

135 *Ibid*.

136 *Ibid* at para 219.

137 *Statute of Westminster 1931* (UK), 22 & 23 Geo V, c 4.

138 *Montana Band*, above note 132 at para 25.

139 *Simon*, above note 14 at para 30.

140 *Montana First Nation v Canada*, 2007 FCA 218 [*Montana First Nation*].

141 *Simon*, above note 14 at para 32.

142 *Ibid*.

143 *Ibid* at para 33.

144 *Ibid* at para 34.

145 *Ibid* at para 36.

146 *Marshall No 1*, above note 1 at para 16.

147 *Ibid*.

148 *Ibid* at paras 16 and 101.

CHAPTER TWO | On the Interpretation of Treaties

1 *Simon v The Queen*, [1985] 2 SCR 387 at para 30, 24 DLR (4th) 390 [*Simon*].

2 *Quebec (Attorney General) v Moses*, 2010 SCC 17 at para 107 [*Moses*].

3 *R v Marshall*, [1999] 3 SCR 456 at para 78, 177 DLR (4th) 513, McLachlin J, dissenting, but not on this point [*Marshall No 1*] [citations omitted].

4   *R v Sundown*, [1999] 1 SCR 393 at para 24, 170 DLR (4th) 385 [*Sundown*].

5   *Simon*, above note 1 at para 33.

6   *St. Catherine's Milling and Lumber Co v The Queen*, [1888] UKPC 70 at 6, (1888) 58 LJPC 54.

7   *Calder et al v Attorney-General of British Columbia*, [1973] SCR 313 at 328, 34 DLR (3d) 145.

8   *R v Van der Peet*, [1996] 2 SCR 507 at para 49, 137 DLR (4th) 289 [*Van der Peet*].

9   *R v Badger*, [1996] 1 SCR 771 at para 52, 133 DLR (4th) 324 [*Badger*] [citations omitted].

10 *R v Sioui*, [1990] 1 SCR 1025 at 1031, 70 DLR (4th) 427 [*Sioui*] [emphasis added].

11 *Ibid* at 1035.

12 *Ibid* at para 104 (p 1066).

13 *Moses*, above note 2 at para 118, Lebel J, dissenting, but not on this point [emphasis added].

14 *Beckman v Little Salmon/Carmacks First Nation*, 2010 SCC 53 at para 10.

15 *Ibid* at para 10.

16 *Sioui*, above note 10 at 1069.

17 *Badger*, above note 9 at para 39 [emphasis added by the SCC].

18 *Ibid* at paras 72 and 41.

19 *Ibid* at para 41.

20 *Ibid*.

21 *Ibid*.

22 *Manitoba Metis Federation Inc v Canada (Attorney General)*, 2013 SCC 14 at para 82.

23 *Badger*, above note 9 at para 52.

24 *Van der Peet*, above note 8 at para 49.

25 *Ibid* at para 50.

26 *Saugeen First Nation v The Attorney General of Canada*, 2021 ONSC 4181 at para 634 [*Saugeen First Nation*].

27 *Moses*, above note 2 at para 7.

28 *Sioui*, above note 10 at 1069.

29 *Badger*, above note 9 at para 52.

30 *Marshall No 1*, above note 3 at para 14 [citations omitted].

31 See, e.g., *The Queen v George*, [1966] SCR 267, 55 DLR (2d) 386; *R v Lefthand*, 2007 ABCA 206; *Goodswimmer v Canada (Attorney General)*, 2017 ABCA 365.

32 *Van der Peet*, above note 8 at para 120, L'Heureux-Dubé J, dissenting, but not on this point.

33 *Copy of Treaty No. 6 Between Her Majesty the Queen and the Plain and Wood Cree Indians and Other Tribes of Indians at Fort Carlton, Fort Pitt and Battle River with Adhesions*, 23 and 28 August and 9 September 1876, IAND Publication No QS-0574-000-EE-A-1, online: www.rcaanc-cirnac.gc.ca/eng/1100100028710/1581292569426 [*Copy of Treaty No. 6*].

34 *Duke v Puts*, 2004 SKCA 12 at para 9 [*Duke*].

35   *Ibid* at paras 2-4.

36   *Indian Act*, RSC 1985, c I-5.

37   *Sundown*, above note 4 at para 11.

38   *Ibid* at para 33.

39   *Moses*, above note 2 at para 109, Lebel J, dissenting, but not on this point.

40   *Marshall No 1*, above note 3 at para 11 [emphasis added]. See also *Badger*, above note 9 at para 52.

41   *Ibid* [citation omitted].

42   *Marshall No 1*, above note 3 at para 14 [emphasis added].

43   *Moses*, above note 2 at para 7.

44   *Delgamuukw v British Columbia*, [1997] 3 SCR 1010 at para 86, 153 DLR (4th) 193 [*Delgamuukw*].

45   *Ibid* at para 87 [citations omitted].

46   *Saugeen First Nation*, above note 26 at paras 47-49.

47   *R v Khan*, [1990] 2 SCR 531 at para 23 (p 542), 59 CCC (3d) 92.

48   *R v Marshall; R v Bernard*, 2005 SCC 43 at para 68 [*Marshall and Bernard*].

49   *Ibid.*

50   *Delgamuukw*, above note 44 at para 93.

51   *Saugeen First Nation*, above note 26 at para 58.

52   *Marshall and Bernard*, above note 48 at para 68.

53   *Van der Peet*, above note 8 at para 68.

54   *Marshall No 1*, above note 3 at para 5 [emphasis omitted].

55   *Ibid* at paras 19-21.

56   *Ibid* at para 43 [citations omitted.

57   *Ibid* at para 14.

58   Canada, Department of Indian Affairs, *Indian Treaties and Surrenders: From 1680 to 1890*, vol 1 (Ottawa: B Chamberlain, 1891) at 113.

59   *Ibid* at 149.

60   *Copy of Treaty No. 6*, above note 33.

61   Éditeur officiel du Québec, *The James Bay and Northern Québec Agreement*, 11 November 1975 (Quebec: ÉODQ, 1976) at 23-54.

62   *Sioui*, above note 10 at para 111 (p 1068).

63   *Ibid* at para 107 (p 1066-67).

64   *Ibid* at 1068.

65   *Ibid* at para 112 (p 1068).

66   *Ibid* at 1071.

67   *Mikisew Cree First Nation v Canada (Minister of Canadian Heritage)*, 2005 SCC 69 at para 46.

68   *Ibid* at para 45.

69   *Ibid* at para 47.

CHAPTER THREE | On the Fulfillment of Treaties

1   *Mikisew Cree First Nation v Canada (Minister of Canadian Heritage)*, 2005 SCC 69 at para 2 [*Mikisew Cree*]. See also para 52.

2   *R v Marshall*, [1999] 3 SCR 456 at para 17, 177 DLR (4th) 513 [*Marshall No 1*].

3   *Ibid.*

4   *Ibid* at para 23.

5   *Ibid* at para 16.

6   *R v Badger*, [1996] 1 SCR 771 at para 9, 133 DLR (4th) 324 [*Badger*].

7   *Ibid* at para 41.

8   *Manitoba Metis Federation Inc v Canada (Attorney General)*, 2013 SCC 14 at para 65 [*Manitoba Metis Federation*].

9   *Guerin v The Queen*, [1984] 2 SCR 335, 13 DLR (4th) 321 [*Guerin*].

10 John J. Borrows & Leonard I. Rotman, *Aboriginal Legal Issues: Cases, Materials & Commentary*, 5th ed (Toronto: LexisNexis, 2018) at 11.

11 Brian Slattery, "Aboriginal Rights and the Honour of the Crown" (2005) 29:20 *Supreme Court Law Review* (2d) 433 at 445. See also *Manitoba Metis Federation*, above note 8 at para 66; *Haida Nation v British Columbia (Minister of Forests)*, 2004 SCC 73 at para 32 [*Haida Nation*].

12 David Arnot, "Treaties as a Bridge to the Future" (2001) 50 *University of New Brunswick Law Journal* 57 at 65–66.

13 *Province of Ontario v The Dominion of Canada and the Province of Quebec* (1895), 25 SCR 434 at 512.

14 *Marshall No 1*, above note 2 at para 50.

15 *The Queen v George*, [1966] SCR 267, 55 DLR (2d) 386.

16 *Ibid* at 279.

17 *R v Sparrow*, [1990] 1 SCR 1075, 70 DLR (4th) 385 [*Sparrow*].

18 *Guerin*, above note 9 at 386–87.

19 *Sparrow*, above note 17 at para 62 (p 1109).

20 *Wewaykum Indian Band v Canada*, 2002 SCC 79 at para 81 [*Wewaykum*].

21 *Badger*, above note 6 at para 41.

22 *Manitoba Metis Federation*, above note 8 at para 68.

23 *Ibid* at para 72.

24 *Act respecting the Makivik Corporation*, CQLR, c S-18.1. Although the statute uses the spelling "Makivik," the corporation itself uses the spelling "Makivvik."

25 *Haida Nation*, above note 11. Although *Haida Nation* does not involve treaty rights, the duty to consult and accommodate that arises from the decision has been held to apply to treaty rights, per *Mikisew Cree*, above note 1 at paras 44, 56–57.

26 *Rio Tinto Alcan Inc v Carrier Sekani Tribal Council*, 2010 SCC 43 [*Rio Tinto Alcan*].

27 *Manitoba Metis Federation*, above note 8 at para 73 (p 1110) [emphasis in original].

28 *Sparrow*, above note 17 at para 64.

29 *Badger*, above note 6 at para 73.

30 *Haida Nation*, above note 11 at para 32.

31 *Manitoba Metis Federation*, above note 8 at para 9.

32 *Saugeen First Nation v The Attorney General of Canada*, 2021 ONSC 4181 at para 80 [*Saugeen First Nation*].

33 *Delgamuukw v British Columbia*, [1997] 3 SCR 1010 at para 145, 153 DLR (4th) 193 [*Delgamuukw*].

34 *Haida Nation*, above note 11 at paras 16–17 [citations omitted].

35 *Manitoba Metis Federation*, above note 8 at para 79.

36 *Ibid* at para 74.

37 *Guerin*, above note 9 at 384.

38 *Manitoba Metis Federation*, above note 8 at para 73.

39 *Guerin*, above note 9 at paras 96–97 (p 383–84).

40 *Alberta v Elder Advocates of Alberta Society*, 2011 SCC 24 at para 44 [*Elder Advocates*].

41 *Wewaykum*, above note 20 at paras 79–83; *Haida Nation*, above note 11 at para 18.

42 *Guerin*, above note 9 at 384, quoting Ernest Weinrib, "The Fiduciary Obligation" (1975) 25:1 *University of Toronto Law Journal* 1 at 7 [emphasis added].

43 *Ibid* at 336.

44 *Marshall No 1*, above note 2 at paras 62–66.

45 *Manitoba Metis Federation*, above note 8 at para 53 [emphasis added].

46 *R v Van der Peet*, [1996] 2 SCR 507 at paras 49–75, 137 DLR (4th) 289 [*Van der Peet*].

47 *R v Powley*, 2003 SCC 43 at paras 16–17.

48 *Wewaykum*, above note 20 at para 86.

49 *Ibid* at para 92 [citations omitted].

50 *Ibid* at para 97.

51 *Elder Advocates*, above note 40 at para 43.

52 Bryan Birtles, "Another Inappropriate F Word: Fiduciary Doctrine and the Crown-Indigenous Relationship in Canada" (2020) 9:1 *American Indian Law Journal* 1 at 2.

53 *Guerin*, above note 9 at 384.

54 *Wewaykum*, above note 20 at paras 86 and 100.

55 *Southwind v Canada*, 2021 SCC 28 at para 1 [*Southwind*].

56 *Ibid* at paras 5–6.

57 *Ibid* at paras 10–11.

58 *Ibid* at para 11.

59 *Ibid* at para 12.

60 *Williams Lake Indian Band v Canada (Aboriginal Affairs and Northern Development)*, 2018 SCC 4 at para 1 [*Williams Lake Indian Band*].

61 *Ibid* at paras 10–13.

62 *Ibid* at para 14.

63 *Ibid* at para 17.

64 *Ibid* at para 54.

65 *British Columbia Terms of Union* (UK), 1871, reprinted in RSC 1985, Appendix II, No 10.

66 *Williams Lake Indian Band*, above note 60 at para 55 [citations omitted].

67 *R v Gladstone*, [1996] 2 SCR 723 at para 63, 137 DLR (4th) 648.

68 *Ibid* [citations omitted].

69 *Williams Lake Indian Band*, above note 60 at para 100.

70 *Haida Nation*, above note 11; *Rio Tinto Alcan*, above note 26.

71 *Mikisew Cree*, above note 1.

72 *Beckman v Little Salmon/Carmacks First Nation*, 2010 SCC 53.

73 *Haida Nation*, above note 11 at para 35 [citation omitted].

74 *Rio Tinto Alcan*, above note 26 at para 31.

75 *Ibid* at para 40 [citation omitted].

76 *Rio Tinto Alcan*, above note 26 at para 42 [emphasis added].

77 *Ibid* at paras 43–44.

78 *Mikisew Cree First Nation v Canada (Governor General in Council)*, 2018 SCC 40 at paras 32–35.

79 *Ibid* at para 55, Abella J, concurring in the result, but dissenting on this point.

80 *Rio Tinto Alcan*, above note 26 at para 43.

81 *Constitution Act, 1982*, being Schedule B to the *Canada Act 1982* (UK), 1982, c 11, s 52.

82 *Rio Tinto Alcan*, above note 26 at para 45.

83 *Ibid* at para 46 [citation omitted].

84 *Ibid* at para 47 [citation omitted, emphasis in original].

85 *Haida Nation*, above note 11 at para 43.

86 *Ibid* at para 44.

87 *Ibid* at para 45.

88 *Ibid*.

89 *Mikisew Cree*, above note 1 at para 56.

90 *Ibid* at para 64 [emphasis in original].

91 *Ibid* [emphasis added].

92 *Haida Nation*, above note 11 at para 44.

93 *Ibid* at para 45.

94 *Ibid* at para 43.

95 *Ibid* at para 53.

96 *Constitution Act, 1867* (UK), 30 & 31 Vict, c 3, s 91(24), reprinted in RSC 1985, Appendix II, No 5.

97 *Ibid* at paras 58–59. See also *Delgamuukw*, above note 33 at paras 173–76.

98 *Haida Nation*, above note 11 at para 32.

99 *Rio Tinto Alcan*, above note 26 at para 31.

100 *Haida Nation*, above note 11 at para 47 [emphasis added].

101 *Haida Nation*, above note 11 at para 42 [citations omitted].

102 *Ktunaxa Nation v British Columbia (Forests, Lands and Natural Resource Operations)*, 2017 SCC 54 at para 5.

103 *Ibid* at para 6.

104 *Ibid* at para 87.

105 *Ibid* at para 115.

106 *Ibid* at para 78.

107 *Badger*, above note 6 at para 41.

108 *Mikisew Cree*, above note 1 at para 51.

109 *Manitoba Metis Federation*, above note 8 at para 79.

110 *Quebec (Attorney General) v Moses*, 2010 SCC 17 at para 23.

111 *Manitoba Metis Federation*, above note 8 at para 75.

112 *Ibid* at para 77.

113 *Marshall No 1*, above note 2 at para 52.

114 *Ibid* at para 51. See also *Badger*, above note 6 at para 41; *Sparrow*, above note 17 at para 57 (p 1107); *R v White*, [1964] 50 DLR (2d) 613 at para 86, 52 WWR (ns) 193 at 221.

115 *Manitoba Metis Federation*, above note 8 at para 80.

116 *Saugeen First Nation*, above note 32 at paras 909-10.

117 *Ibid* at para 918.

118 *Ibid*.

119 *Manitoba Metis Federation*, above note 8 at para 83 [emphasis added].

120 *Ibid* at para 82.

121 *Badger*, above note 6 at para 70.

122 *Ibid* at para 31.

123 *Badger*, above note 6 at para 75.

124 *Mikisew Cree*, above note 1 at para 44.

125 *Marshall No 1*, above note 2 at para 78, McLachlin J, dissenting, although not on this point) [citations omitted].

126 *Badger*, above note 6 at para 46; *R v Horseman*, [1990] 1 SCR 901 at paras 64-68 (p 933-35), [1990] 3 CNLR 95.

127 *Sparrow*, above note 17 at 1099 [emphasis added].

128 *Badger*, above note 6 at para 41.

129 *Ibid* at para 48.

130 *Sparrow,* above note 17 at 1113.

131 *Badger*, above note 6 at para 73.

132 *Sparrow*, above note 17 at para 78 (p 1116).

133 *Marshall No 1*, above note 2 at para 64 [citations omitted].

134 *R v Adams*, [1996] 3 SCR 101 at paras 53-54, 138 DLR (4th) 657.

135 *Badger*, above note 6 at paras 89-90.

136 *Mikisew Cree*, above note 1 at para 44.

137 *Sparrow*, above note 17 at 1119.

138 *Rio Tinto Alcan*, above note 26 at para 31.

139 *Ibid* at para 40.

140 *Badger*, above note 6 at para 79.

141 *Sparrow*, above note 17 at para 71 (p 1113).

142 *Ibid* at para 75 (p 1114).

143 *Ibid* at 1113.

144 *Ibid*.

145 *Ibid* at paras 75–78 (p 1114–16).

146 *Ibid* at para 82 (p 1119).

147 *R v Gladstone*, [1996] 2 SCR 723 at para 73, 137 DLR (4th) 648.

148 *Canadian Charter of Rights and Freedoms*, Part I of the *Constitution Act, 1982*, being Schedule B to the *Canada Act 1982* (UK), 1982, c 11 [*Charter*].

149 *Van der Peet*, above note 46 at para 308, McLachlin J, dissenting.

150 *Ibid*, McLachlin J, dissenting.

151 *Ibid*, McLachlin J, dissenting.

152 *Badger*, above note 6 at para 82 [emphasis added].

CHAPTER FOUR | **On the Breach of Treaties**

1 *Jim Shot Both Sides v Canada*, 2019 FC 789.

2 *Ibid* at para 7.

3 *Ibid* at para 6.

4 *Ibid* at paras 373–79.

5 *Restoule v Canada (Attorney General)*, 2021 ONCA 779 at para 64 [*Restoule*].

6 *Ibid* at para 61 [emphasis added].

7 *Ibid* at para 67.

8 *Ibid* at para 86.

9 *Ibid* at para 70 [footnotes omitted].

10 *Ibid* at paras 71 and 87.

11 *Saugeen First Nation v The Attorney General of Canada*, 2021 ONSC 4181 at para 700 [*Saugeen First Nation*].

12 *Ibid* at para 1006.

13 *Ibid* at para 908.

14 *Nunavut Tunngavik Incorporated v Canada (Attorney General)*, 2014 NUCA 2 at para 9.

15 *Ibid*.

16 *Ibid* at para 17.

17 *Ibid* at paras 17–18.

18 *Ibid* at para 17.

19 *Yahey v British Columbia*, 2021 BCSC 1287 at paras 184–85 [*Yahey*].

20 *Ibid* at para 1116.

21 *Ibid* at para 516, citing *Mikisew Cree First Nation v Canada (Minister of Canadian Heritage)*, 2005 SCC 69 at paras 31 and 48 [*Mikisew Cree*].

22 *Yahey*, above note 19 at para 533.

23 *Ibid* at para 540.

24 *Ibid* [emphasis in original].

25 *Manitoba Metis Federation Inc v Canada (Attorney General)*, 2013 SCC 14 at para 154 [*Manitoba Metis Federation*].

26 *Ibid* at paras 14–18. For the *Manitoba Act*, see *Manitoba Act*, 1870, SC 1870, c 3, reprinted in RSC 1985, App II, No 8.

27 *Ibid* at para 143.

28 *Ibid.*

29 *Ibid* at para 140. It should be noted that the Court rejected the Crown's laches defence for similar reasons: see para 153.

30 *R v Sioui*, [1990] 1 SCR 1025, 70 DLR (4th) 427 [*Sioui*].

31 *Ibid* at para 92.

32 *Constitution Act, 1982*, being Schedule B to the *Canada Act 1982* (UK), 1982, c 11.

33 *Saugeen First Nation*, above note 11 at paras 928–29.

34 *R v Wolfe* (1995), 129 DLR (4th) 58 at 1, [1995] 4 CNLR 99 (Sask CA) [*Wolfe*].

35 *Ibid* at 11.

36 *Ibid* [emphasis in original].

37 *Indian Act*, RSC 1985, c I-5.

38 *Wolfe*, above note 34 at para 36.

39 *Ibid* at para 42.

40 *Ibid* at 22–23.

41 *Southwind v Canada*, 2021 SCC 28 at para 67 [*Southwind*].

42 *Canson Enterprises Ltd v Boughton & Co*, [1991] 3 SCR 534 at para 84 (p 556), 85 DLR (4th) 129 [*Canson Enterprises*].

43 *Southwind*, above note 41 at para 73.

44 *Restoule*, above note 5 at para 54.

45 *Restoule v Canada (Attorney General)*, 2018 ONSC 7701 at para 447 [emphasis added].

46 *Restoule*, above note 5 at para 230.

47 Jeffrey Berryman, *The Law of Equitable Remedies*, 2d ed (Toronto: Irwin Law, 2013) at 480.

48 *Southwind*, above note 41 at para 71, quoting *AIB Group (UK) Plc v Mark Redler & Co Solicitors*, [2014] UKSC 58 at para 83.

49 *Beardy's and Okemasis Band #96 and #97 v Her Majesty the Queen in Right of Canada*, 2016 SCTC 15 at para 75 [*Beardy's*].

50 *R v Badger*, [1996] 1 SCR 771 at para 41, 133 DLR (4th) 324; *Sioui*, above note 30 at para 96 (p 1063); *Simon v The Queen*, [1985] 2 SCR 387 at para 48 (p 410), 24 DLR (4th) 390; *R v Sundown*, [1999] 1 SCR 393 at para 24, 170 DLR (4th) 385.

51 *Beardy's*, above note 49 at para 76.

52 *Canson Enterprises*, above note 42 at 543.

53 *Beardy's*, above note 49 at para 77.

54 *Siska Indian Band v Her Majesty the Queen in Right of Canada*, 2021 SCTC 2 at para 60.

55 *Southwind*, above note 41 at para 115.

56 *Canson Enterprises*, above note 42 at paras 55 and 84.

57 *Southwind*, above note 41 at para 83.

58 *Ibid* at para 70.

59 *Canson Enterprises*, above note 42 at para 84 (p 556).

60 *Southwind*, above note 41 at para 73.

61 *Canson Enterprises*, above note 42 at para 61 (p 543).

62 *Southwind*, above note 41 at para 75.

63 *Ibid* at para 124.

64 *Ibid* at para 68, citing *Guerin v The Queen*, [1984] 2 SCR 335 at 360, 13 DLR (4th) 321.

65 *Day v Mead*, [1987] 2 NZLR 443 (CA).

66 *Canson Enterprises*, above note 42 at para 53 (p 585–87).

67 *Ibid* at 545–46 and 543.

68 *Ibid* at 556.

69 *Ibid* at 545.

70 *Ibid*.

71 *Ibid* at 543.

72 This sentence uses the word "typically" purposefully. Justice McLachlin does allow that there may be a limit to a court's refusal to apply principles such as mitigation, writing,

> When the plaintiff, after due notice and opportunity, fails to take the most obvious steps to alleviate his or her losses, then we might rightly say that the plaintiff has been 'the author of his own misfortune.' At this point, the plaintiff's failure to mitigate may become so egregious that it is no longer sensible to say that the losses which followed were caused by the fiduciary's breach. But until that point mitigation will not be required.

Ibid at 554.

73 *Lemberg v Perris*, 2010 ONSC 3690 [*Lemberg*].

74 *Ibid* at para 88 [emphasis added].

75 *Ibid* at para 90.

76 *Southwind v Canada*, 2017 FC 906 at para 233.

77 *Canson Enterprises*, above note 42 at para 61 (p 543).

78 *Southwind*, above note 41 at para 79.

79 *Ibid* at para 129.

80 *Ibid* at para 140.

81 *Ibid* at para 143.

82 *Ibid* at para 83.

83 *Beardy's*, above note 49 at para 30.

84 *Ibid* at para 133.

85 *Whitefish Lake Band of Indians v Canada (Attorney General)*, 2007 ONCA 744 at para 69 [*Whitefish*].

86 *Southwind*, above note 41 at para 98.

87 *Whitefish*, above note 85 at para 69.

88 *Ibid* at para 80.

89 *London Loan & Savings Company of Canada v Brickenden*, [1934] 2 WWR 545, 3 DLR 465 (JCPC).

90 *Southwind*, above note 41 at para 82.

91 *Whitefish*, above note 85 at para 90; see also *Southwind*, above note 41 at para 123.

92 *Southwind*, above note 41 at para 124.

93 *Ibid* at para 123; see also *Whitefish*, above note 85 at para 90.

94 *Canson Enterprises*, above note 42 at 543.

95 *Southwind*, above note 41 at para 123.

96 *Ibid* at para 132.

97 *Ibid*.

98 *Ibid* at para 123.

99 *Whitefish*, above note 85 at para 64.

100 *Southwind*, above note 41 at para 126.

101 *Air Canada v Ontario (Liquor Control Board)*, [1997] 2 SCR 581 at paras 85–86, 148 DLR (4th) 193.

102 *Southwind*, above note 41 at para 132, quoting *Southwind v Canada*, 2019 FCA 171 at para 82.

103 *Southwind*, above note 41 at para 144.

104 *Norberg v Wynrib*, [1992] 2 SCR 226 at 299, 92 DLR (4th) 449, quoting Mark Ellis, *Fiduciary Duties in Canada* (Don Mills, ON: Richard DeBoo, 1988) at 20–24.

105 *Southwind*, above note 41 at para 144.

106 *Ibid* at para 123.

107 *M(K) v M(H)*, [1992] 3 SCR 6 at para 98, 96 DLR (4th) 289.

108 *Ibid* at 77.

109 Graeme Mew, *The Law of Limitations*, 3d ed (Toronto: LexisNexis, 2016) ch 4 at § 2.81.

110 *M(K) v M(H)*, above note 107 (p 78).

111 *KK v GKW*, 2008 ONCA 489.

112 *Manitoba Metis Federation*, above note 25.

113 Mew, above note 109, ch 4 at § 2.77.

114 *Chippewas of Sarnia Band v Canada (Attorney General)* (2000), 195 DLR (4th) 135 at para 267, [2001] 1 CNLR 56 [*Chippewas of Sarnia Band*].

115 *Ling Chi Medicine Co (HK) v Persaud*, [1998] FCJ No 861 at para 3, 81 CPR (3d) 369 (CA).

116 *Specific Claims Tribunal Act*, SC 2008, c 22, s 19.

117 *Canada v Stoney Band*, 2005 FCA 15 at para 20.

118 *Ibid* at para 27; *Wewaykum Indian Band v Canada*, 2002 SCC 79 [*Wewaykum*].

119 *Saugeen First Nation*, above note 11 at para 1156.

120 *Ibid*.

121 *M(K) v M(H)*, above note 107 at para 101 (p 78–79).

122 *Manitoba Metis Federation*, above note 25 at para 147.

123 *M(K) v M(H)*, above note 107 at para 102 (p 79).

124 *Saugeen First Nation*, above note 11 at para 1189.

125 *Chippewas of Sarnia Band*, above note 114 at para 271.

126 *Ibid* at para 272.

127 *Wewaykum*, above note 118 at para 111.

128 *Manitoba Metis Federation*, above note 25 at para 152.

Index

About the Author

Bryan Birtles is a graduate of the University of Alberta and Osgoode Hall Law School, York University. He is a member of the Law Society of Ontario, and the author of a number of academic papers on a variety of topics including Aboriginal law, criminal law, and legal advocacy. Prior to joining the legal profession, he was a journalist and writer in Canada and Northern Ireland. He currently serves as legal counsel to the Specific Claims Tribunal.[1]

---

1   This book represents, solely, the author's opinion and does not necessarily reflect that of the Specific Claims Tribunal.

About the Editor

Gregory Tardi, BCL, LLB, DJur, is the general editor of the Understanding Canada Collection. He is a member of the Barreau du Québec and serves both as president of the Institute of Parliamentary and Political Law and as editor of the *Journal of Parliamentary and Political Law*. He has served as legal counsel with Elections Canada and at the House of Commons. He has taught at McGill, York, and Queen's universities and is the author of several books, including *The Theory and Practice of Political Law* and *Anatomy of an Election*.

Printed in the USA
CPSIA information can be obtained
at www.ICGtesting.com
JSHW012347141124
73596JS00008B/21

9 781552 217306